Viktoriya Yakubouskaya

FLOWERS
Coloring Book
For Adult Relaxation
And Stress Relieving

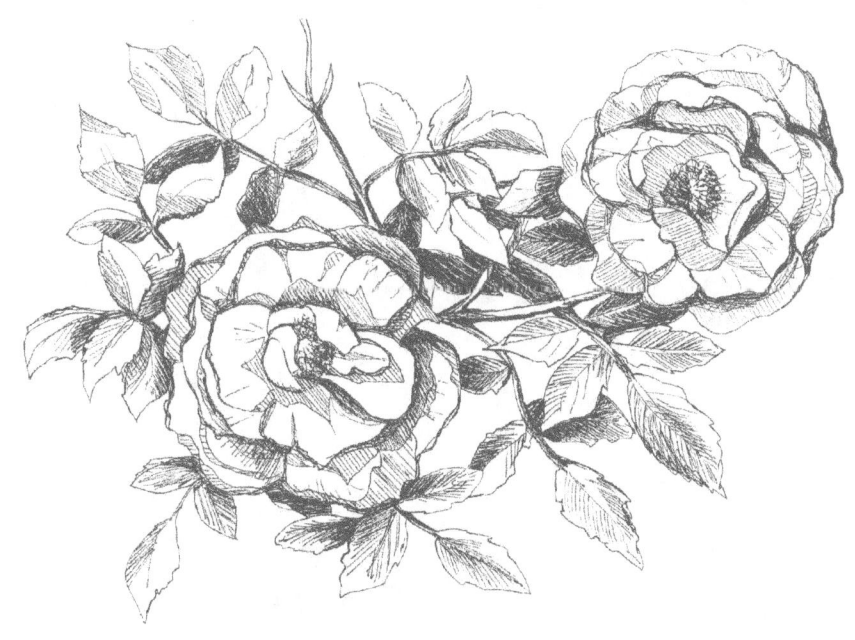

2019

ABOUT

Welcome to my happy and amazing world of color floral designs!

I created something very special for you - Flower Coloring Book For Adult Relaxation... This coloring book contains 48 designs for creativity based on my sketches. You will find flowers such as roses, irises, lilies, phloxes, chamomile, marigold, sunflowers, dahlia, magnolia and more...

I spent many happy hours painting these beautiful flowers that adorn our gardens, and I hope you too will be happy and relaxed while coloring.

The coloring book is suitable for beginner colorists and grayscale coloring lovers. Each design has a name, and you can find online flower images to know exactly which color to use for coloring.

Once completed, you can cut out your favorite design and use it to decorate your bedroom, living or guest room or as a gift to your special person.

So, I invite you to go on an exciting journey with these grayscale flowers.

MY FREE GIFT FOR YOU - Are you a fan of PDF coloring books? Take free PDF Pattern Coloring Book from me here **http://bit.ly/my-books-list**.

Happy color!

Viktoriya Yakubouskaya,
Artist

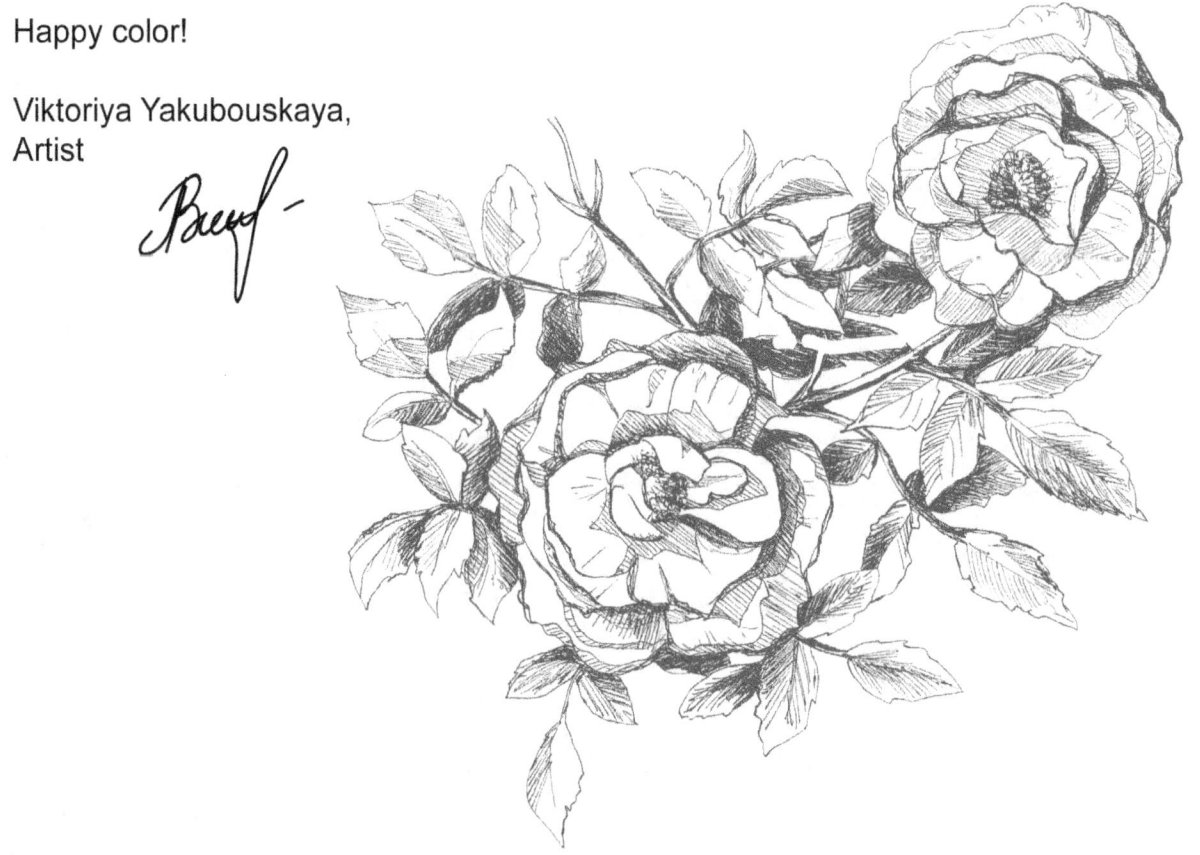

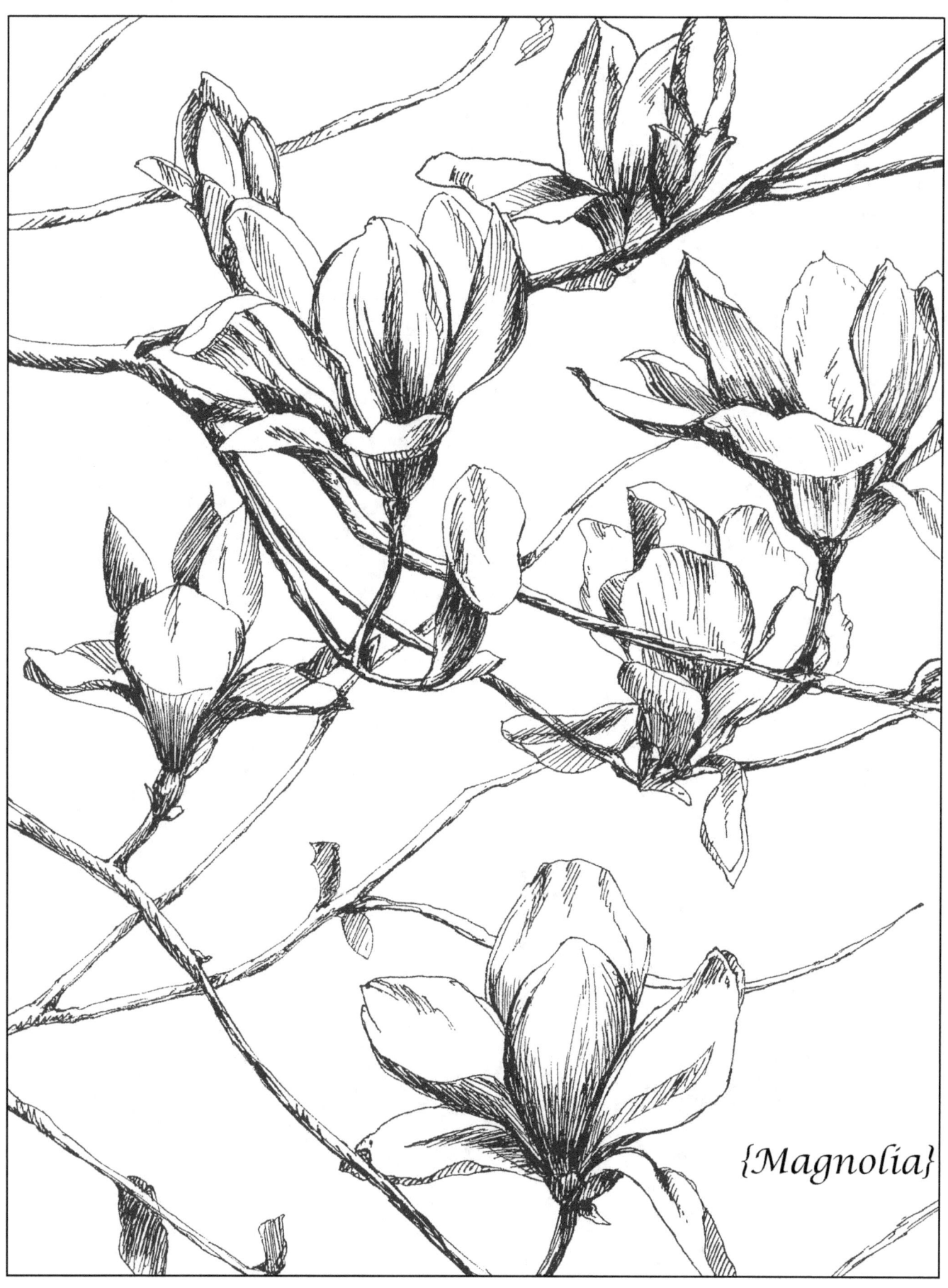

{Magnolia}

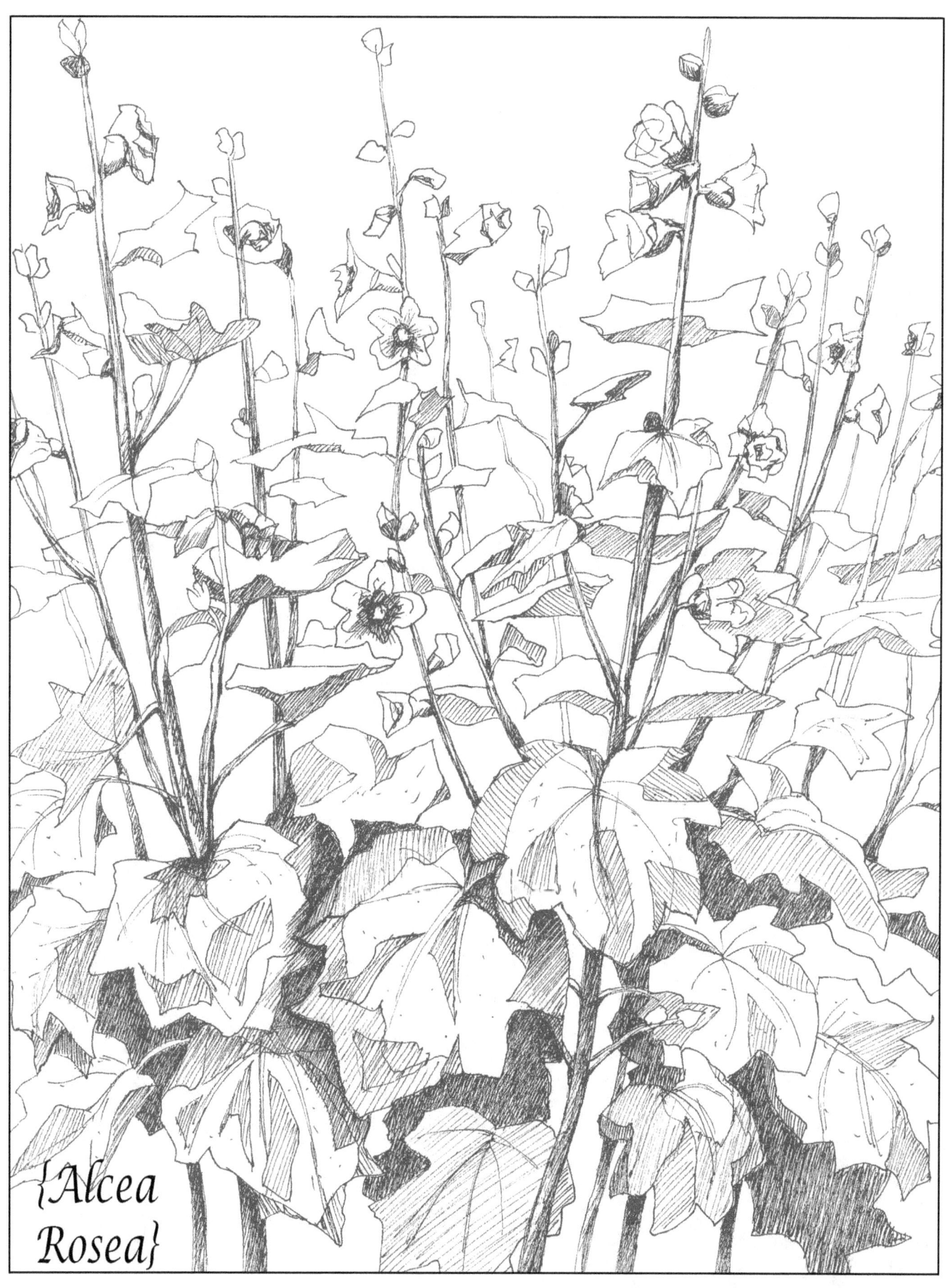

{Alcea
Rosea}

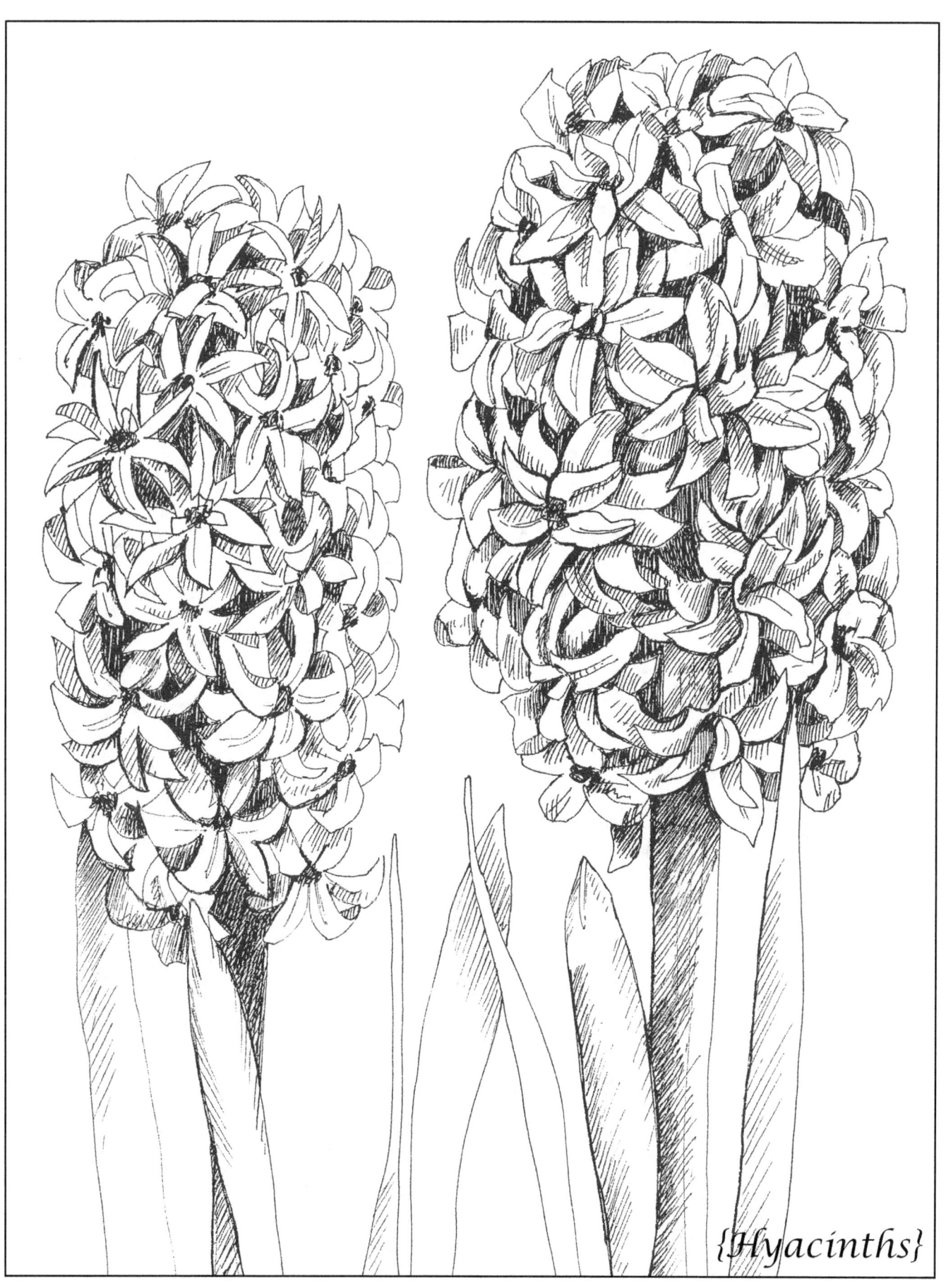

{Hyacinths}

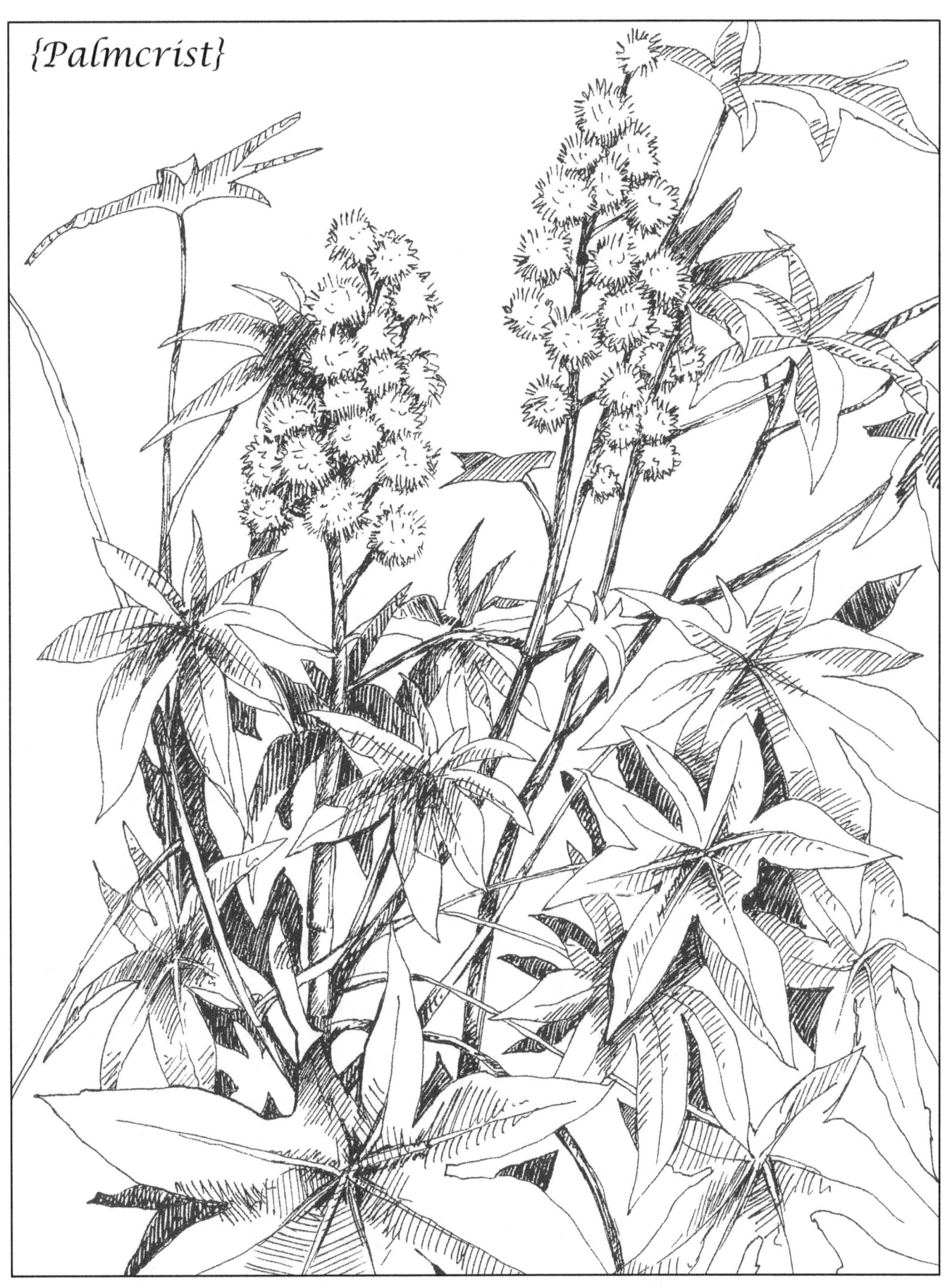

{Palmcrist}

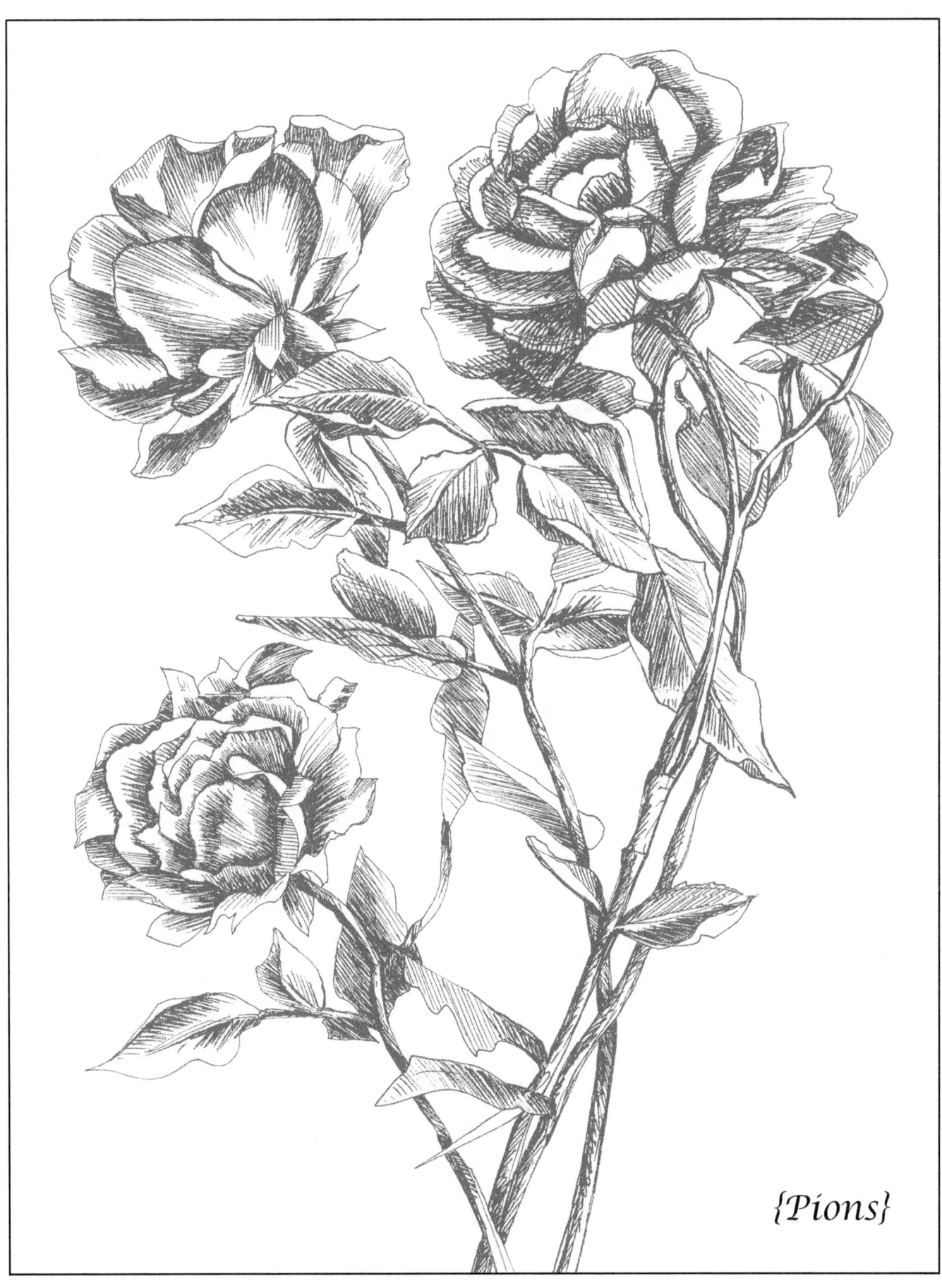

{Pions}

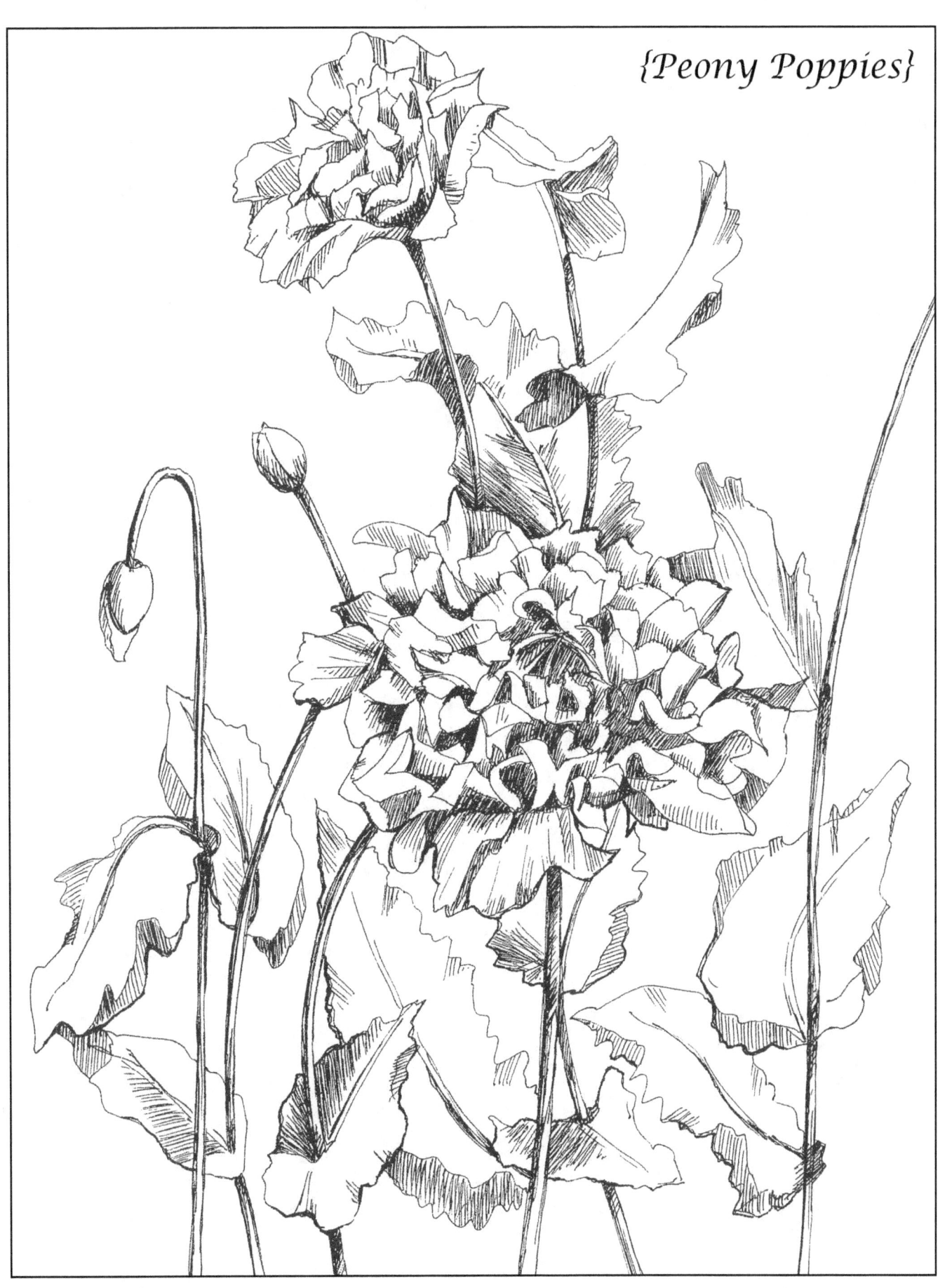

{Peony Poppies}

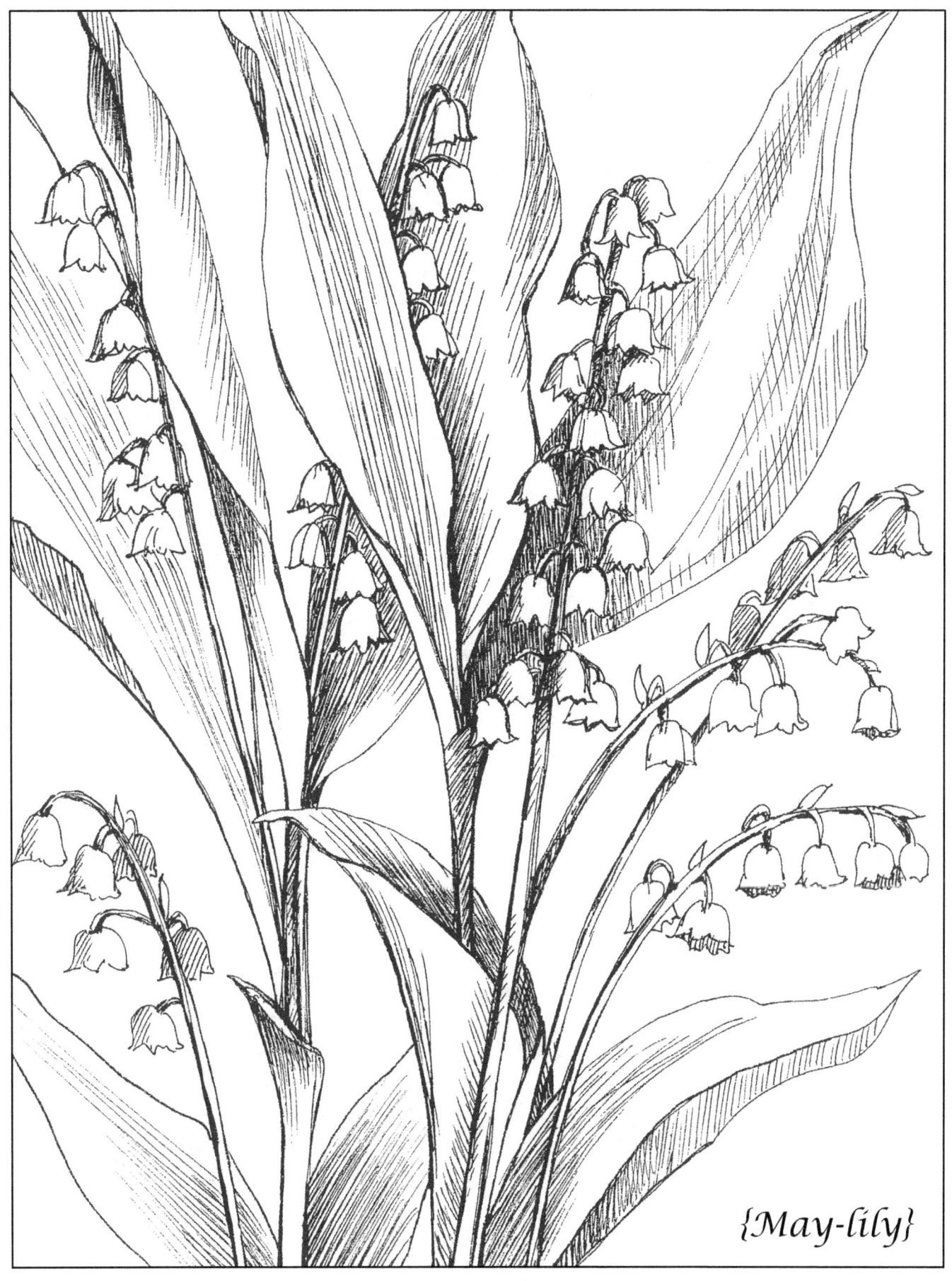

{May-lily}

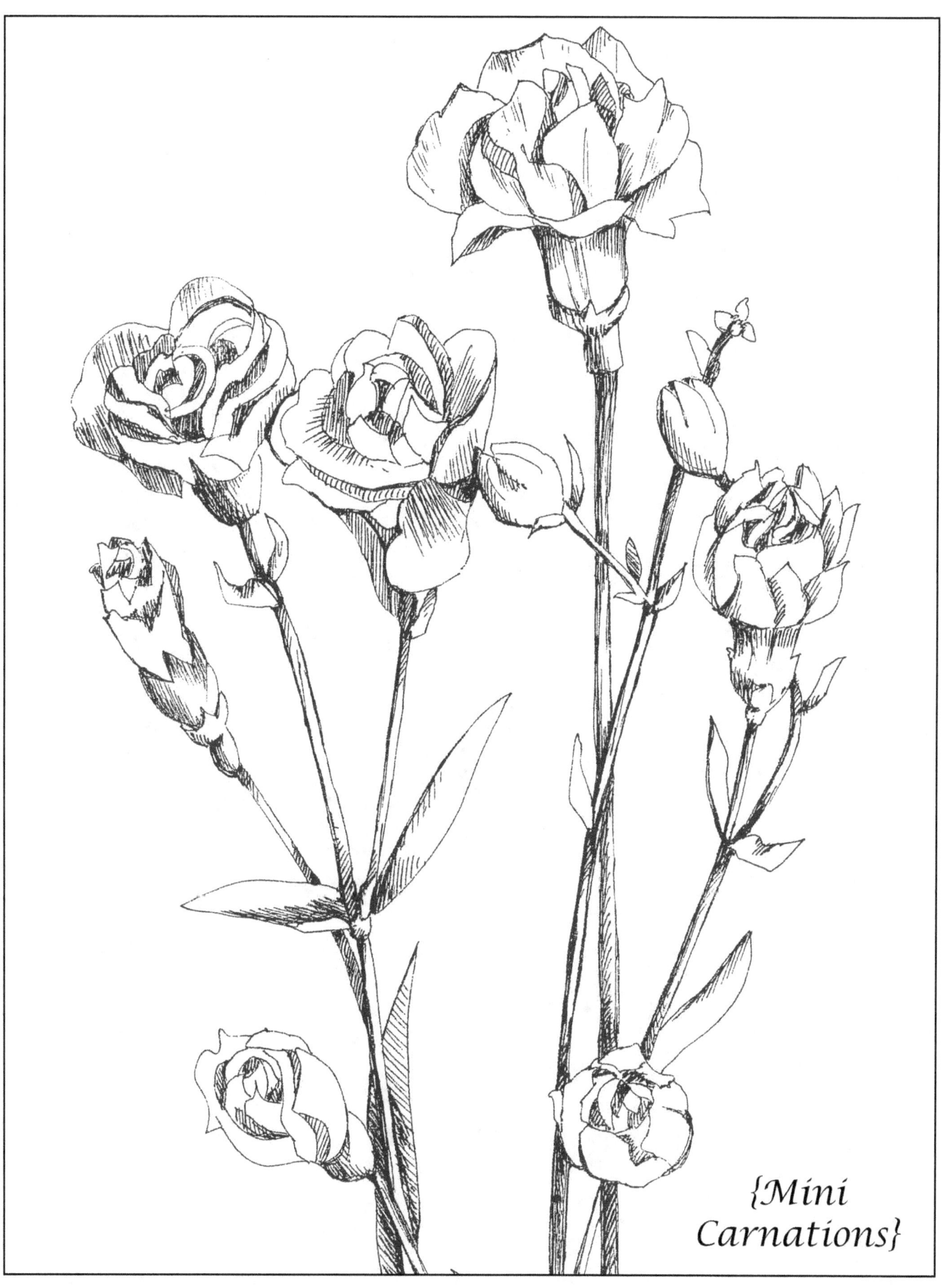

{Mini
Carnations}

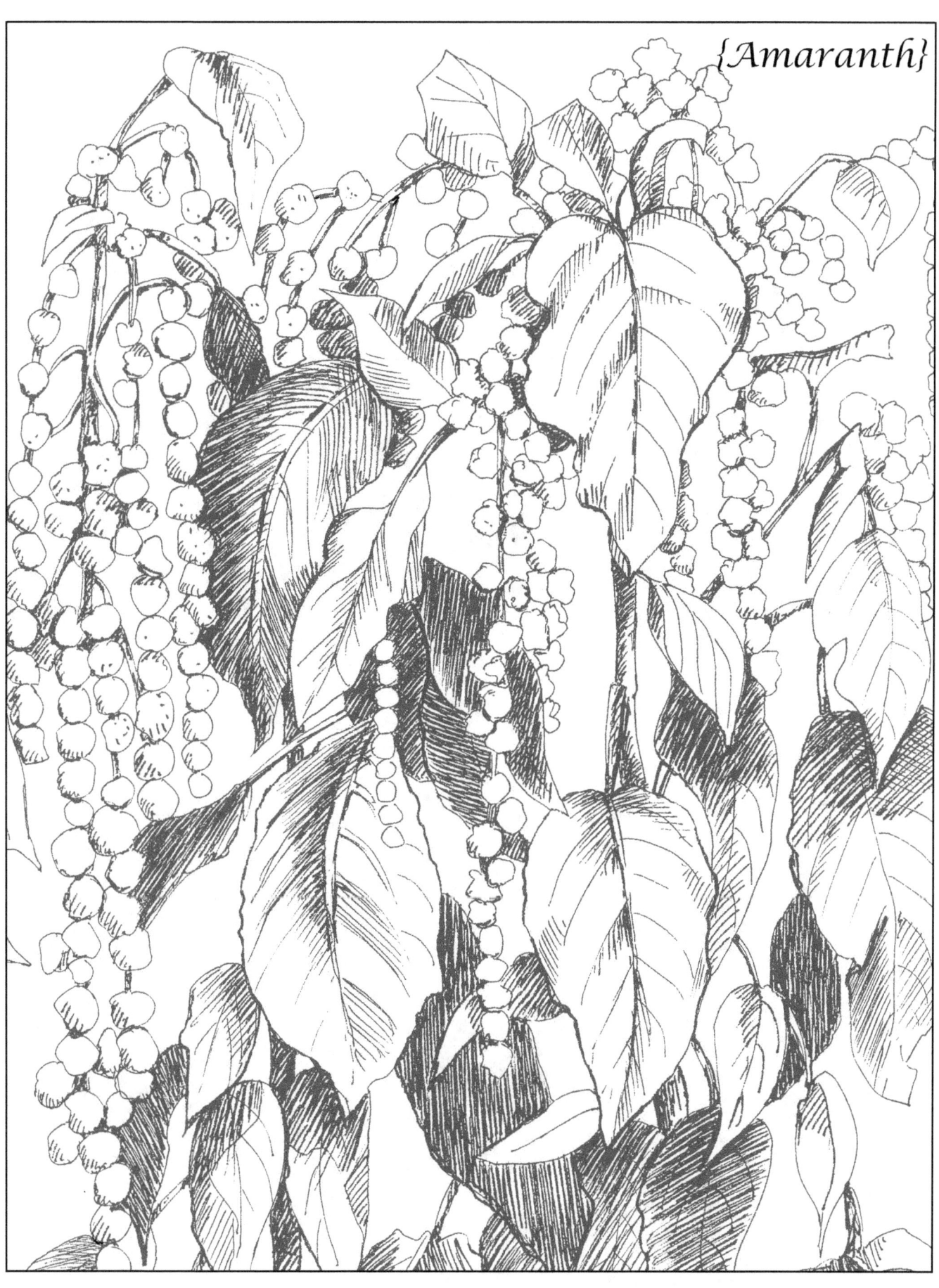

{Amaranth}

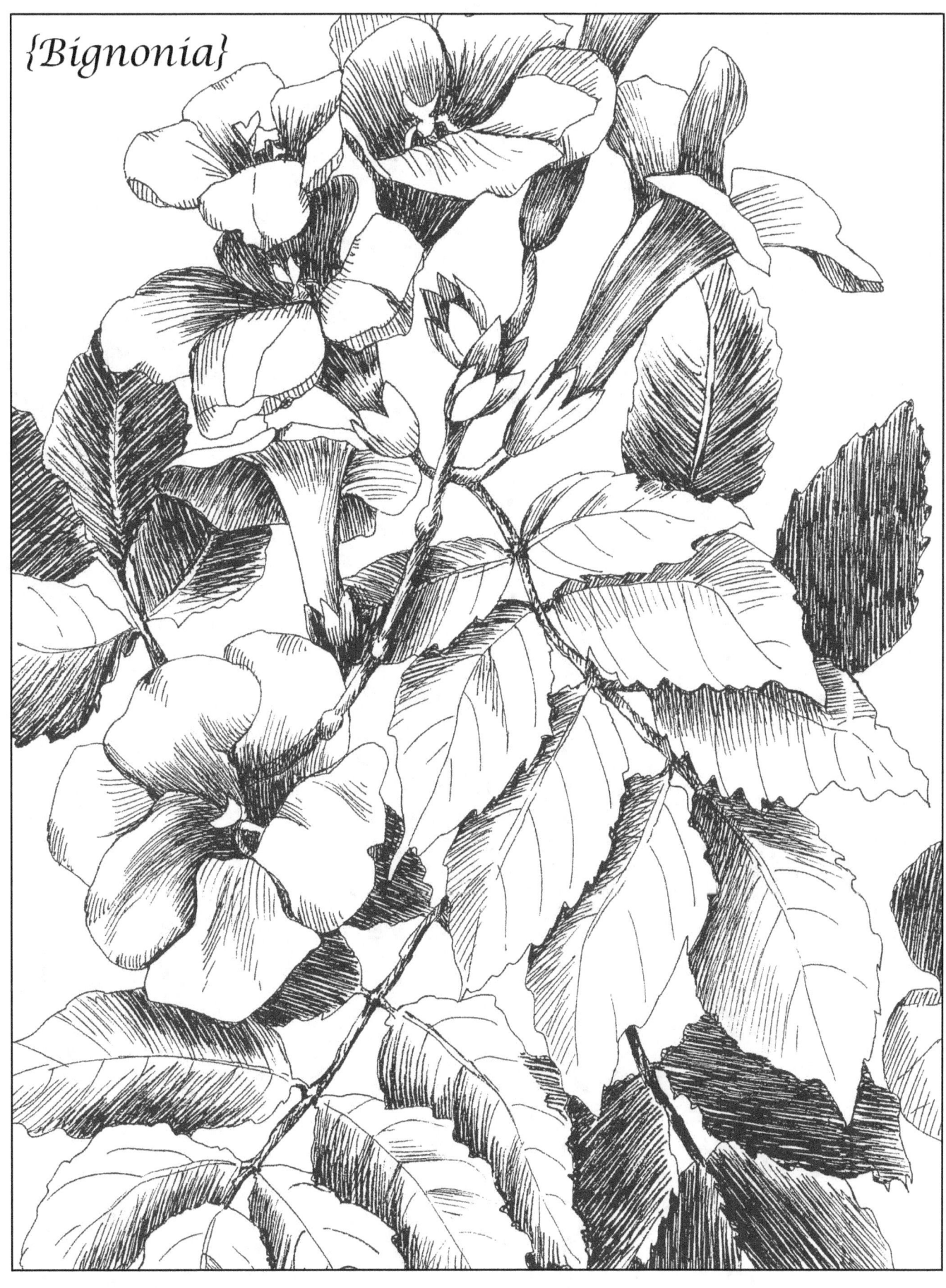

{Bignonia}

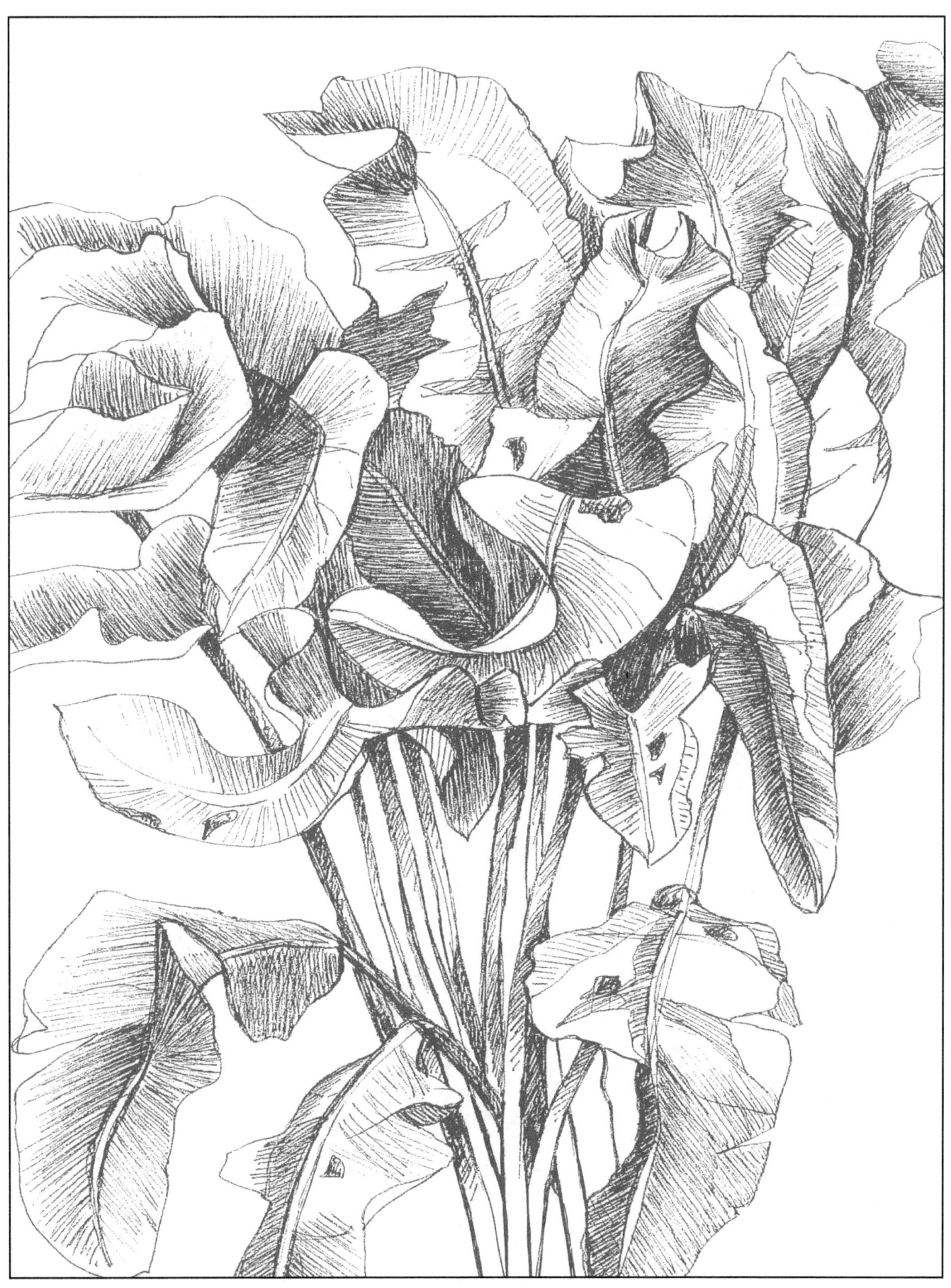

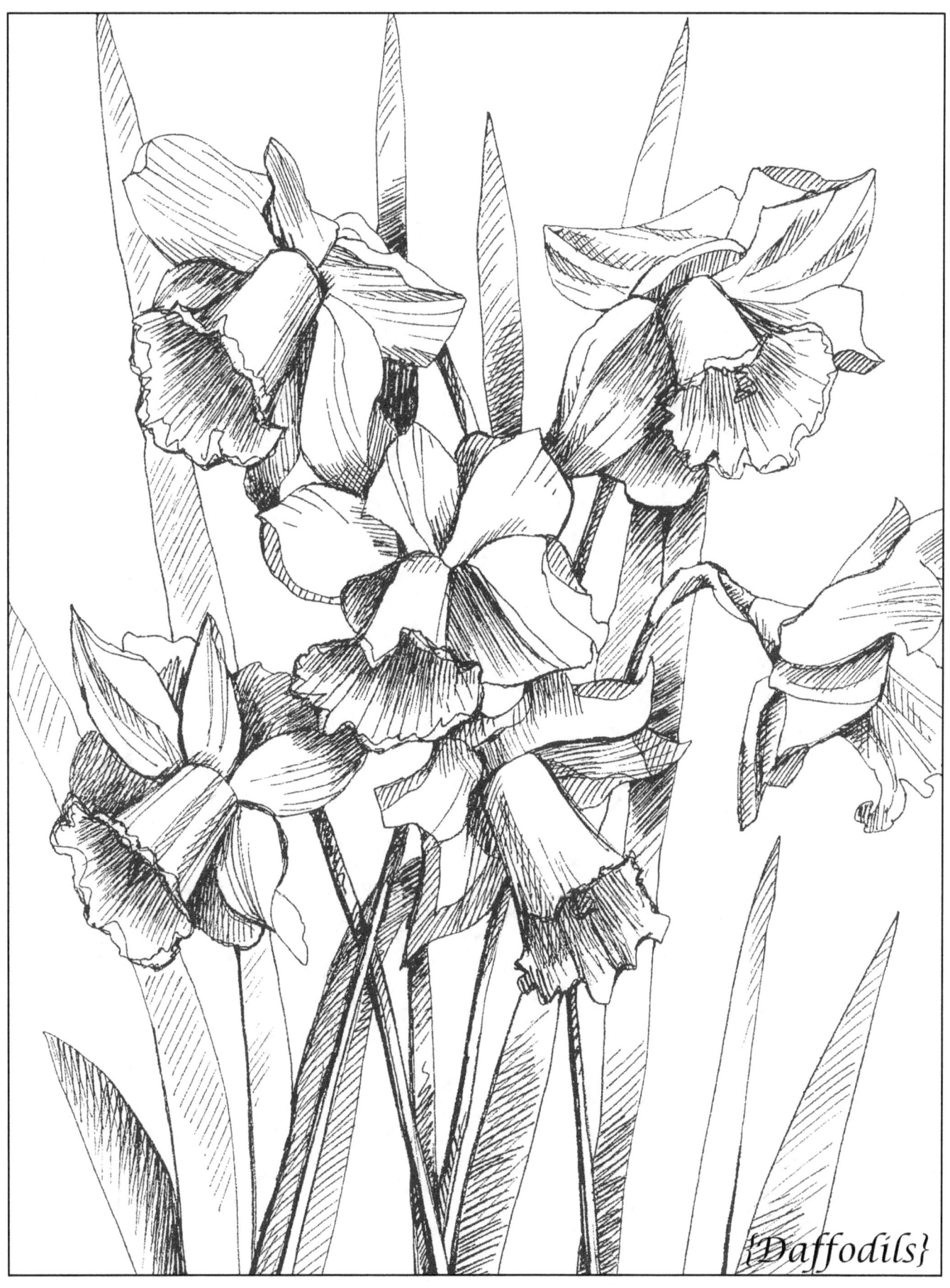

{Daffodils}

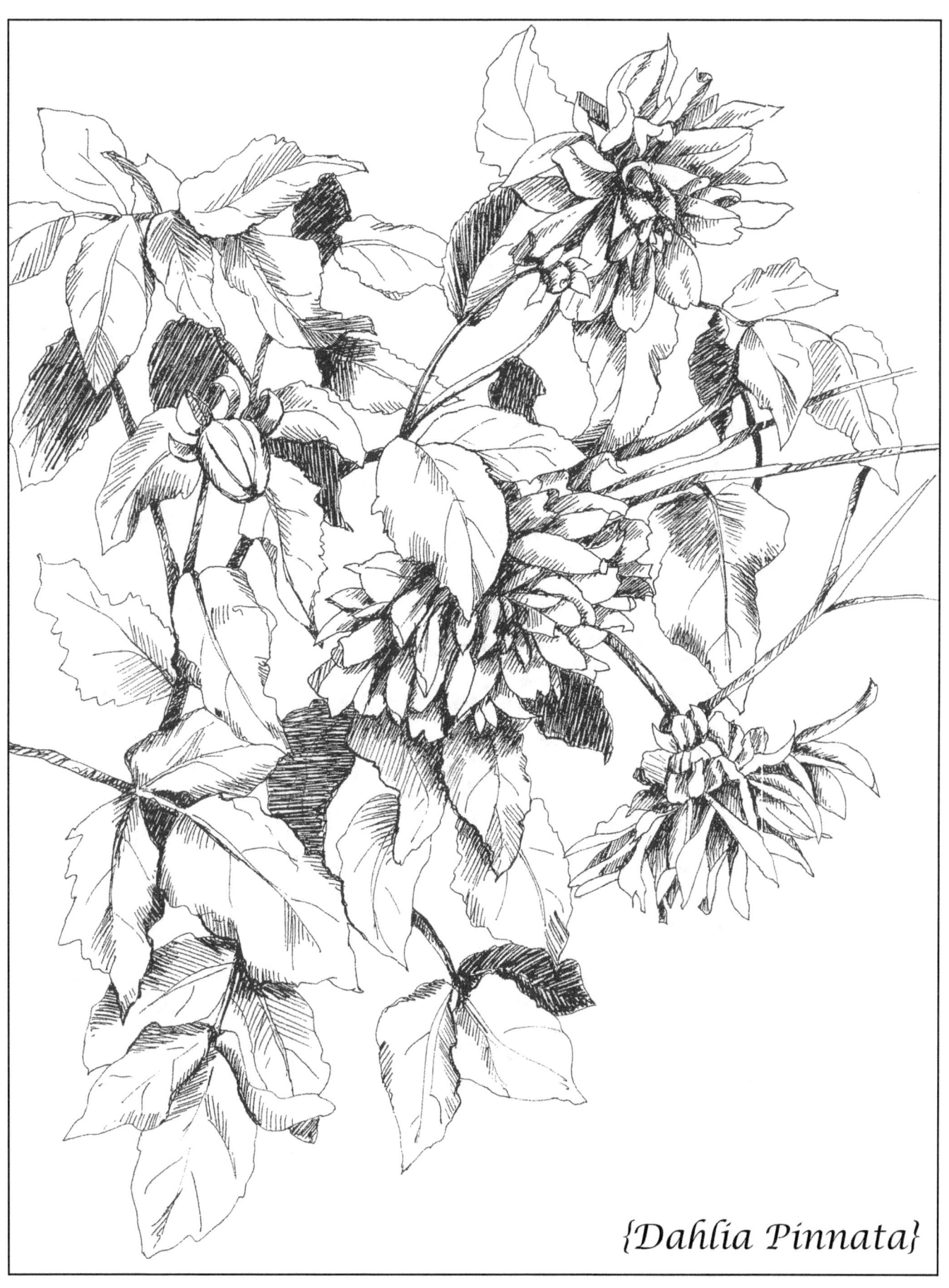

{Dahlia Pinnata}

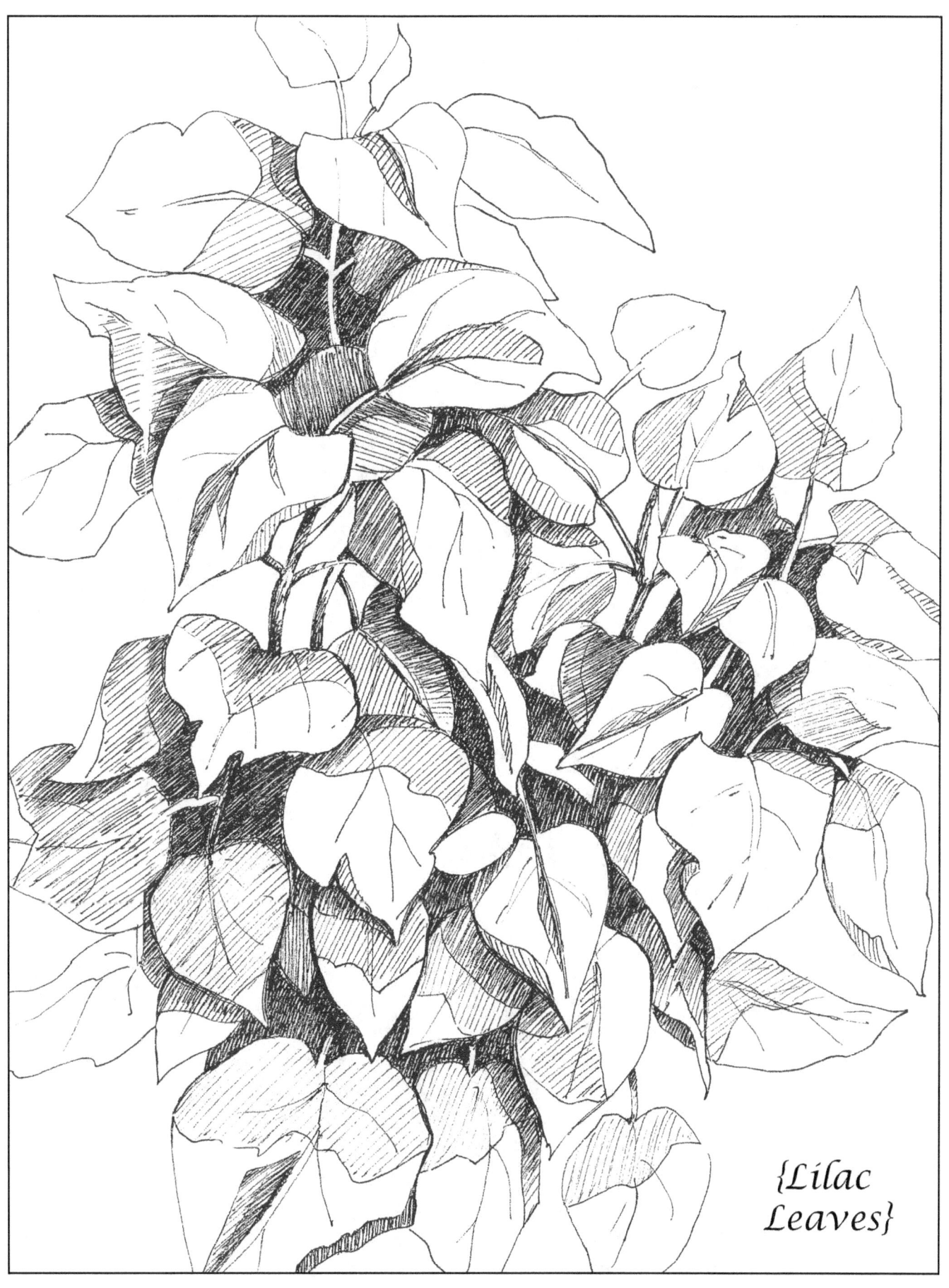

{Lilac
Leaves}

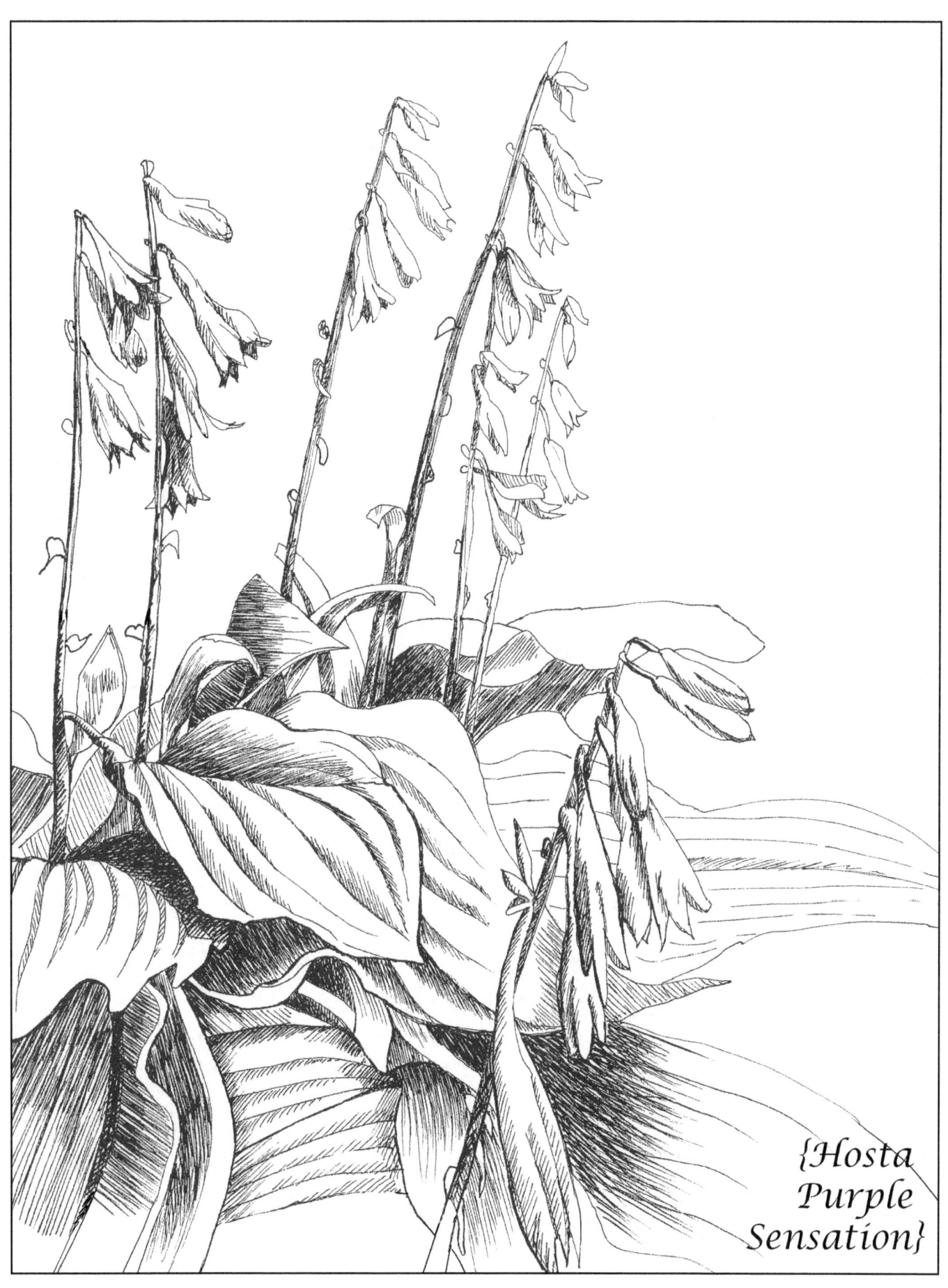

{Hosta
Purple
Sensation}

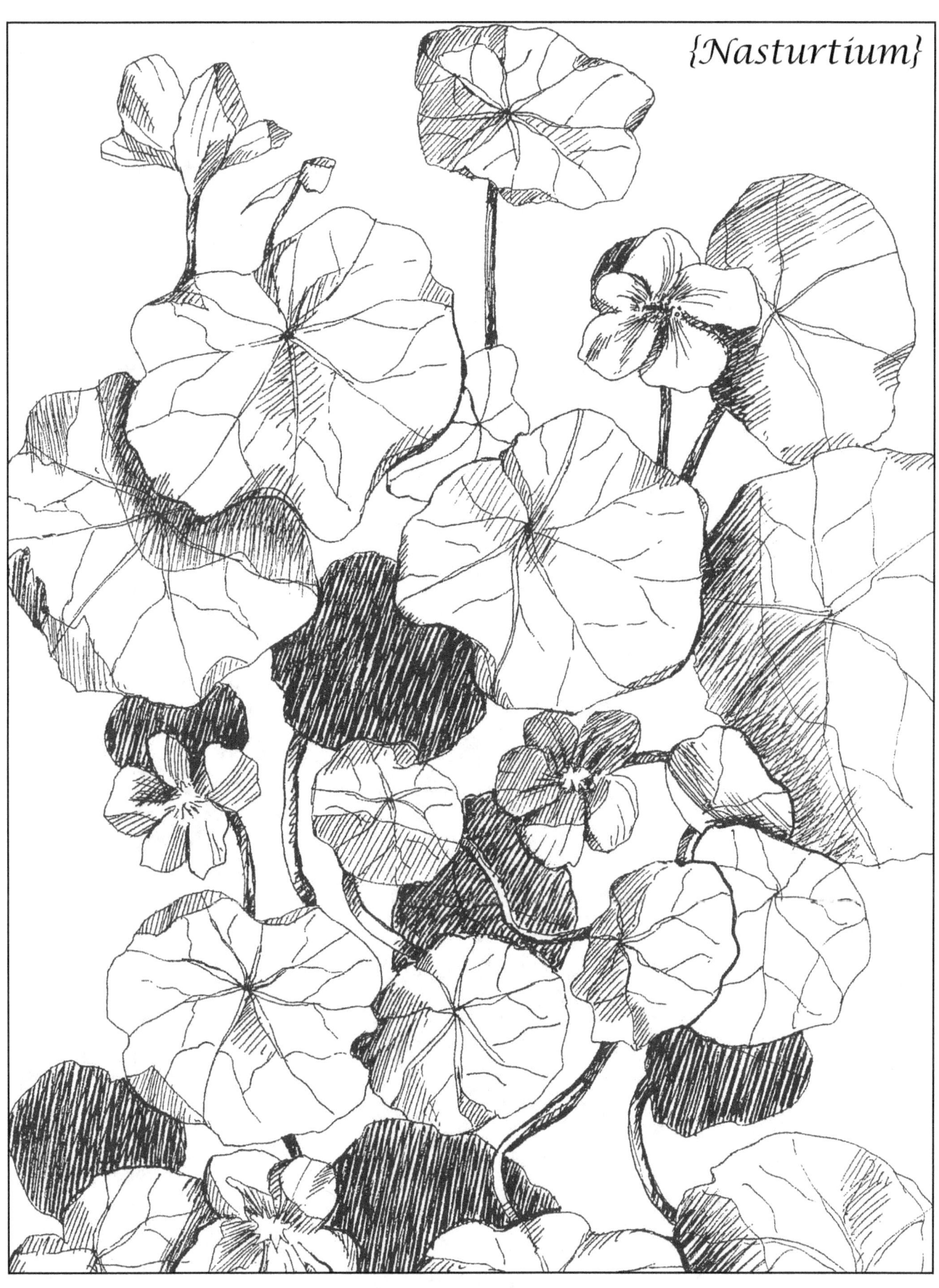

{Nasturtium}

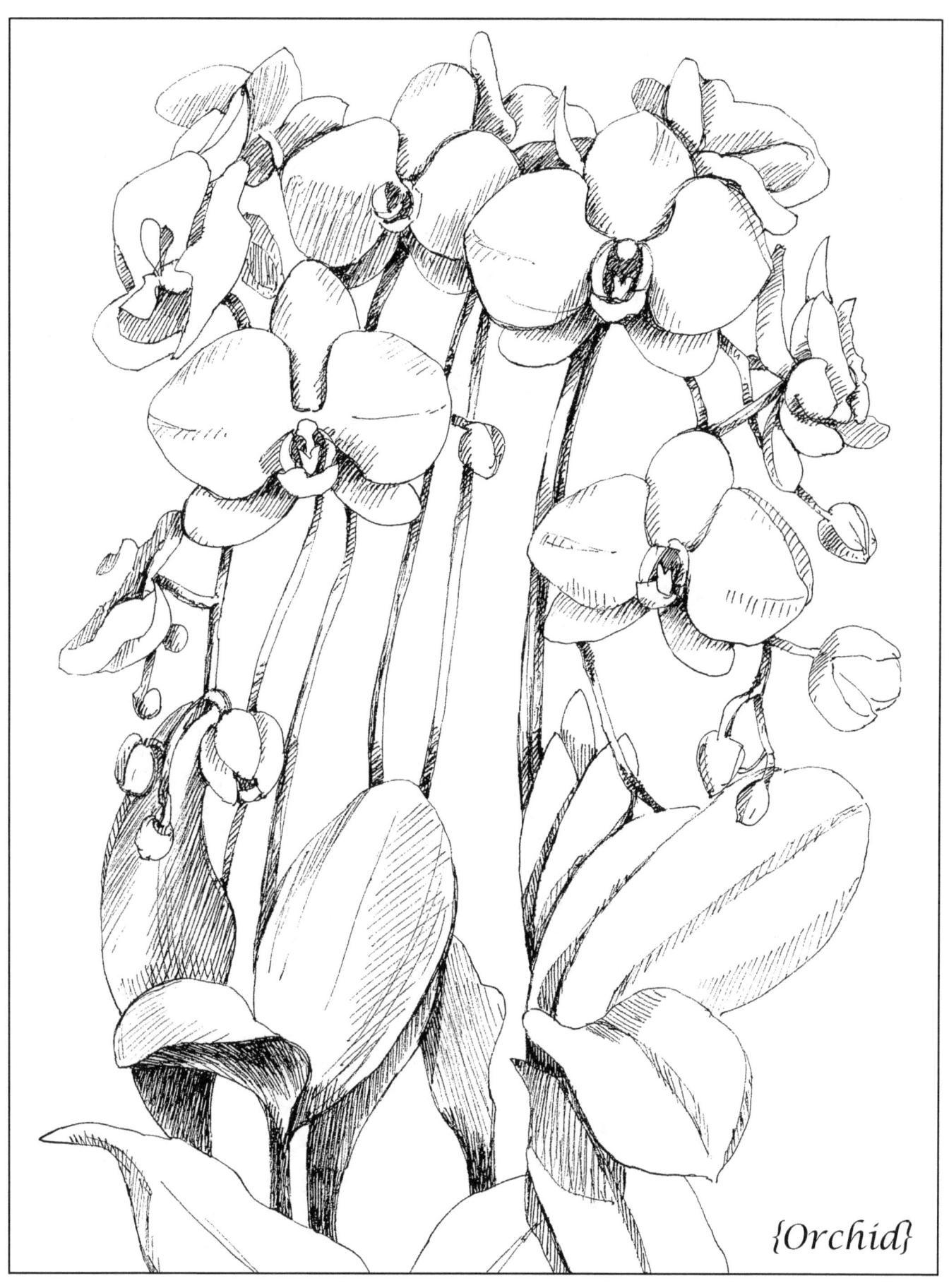

{Orchid}

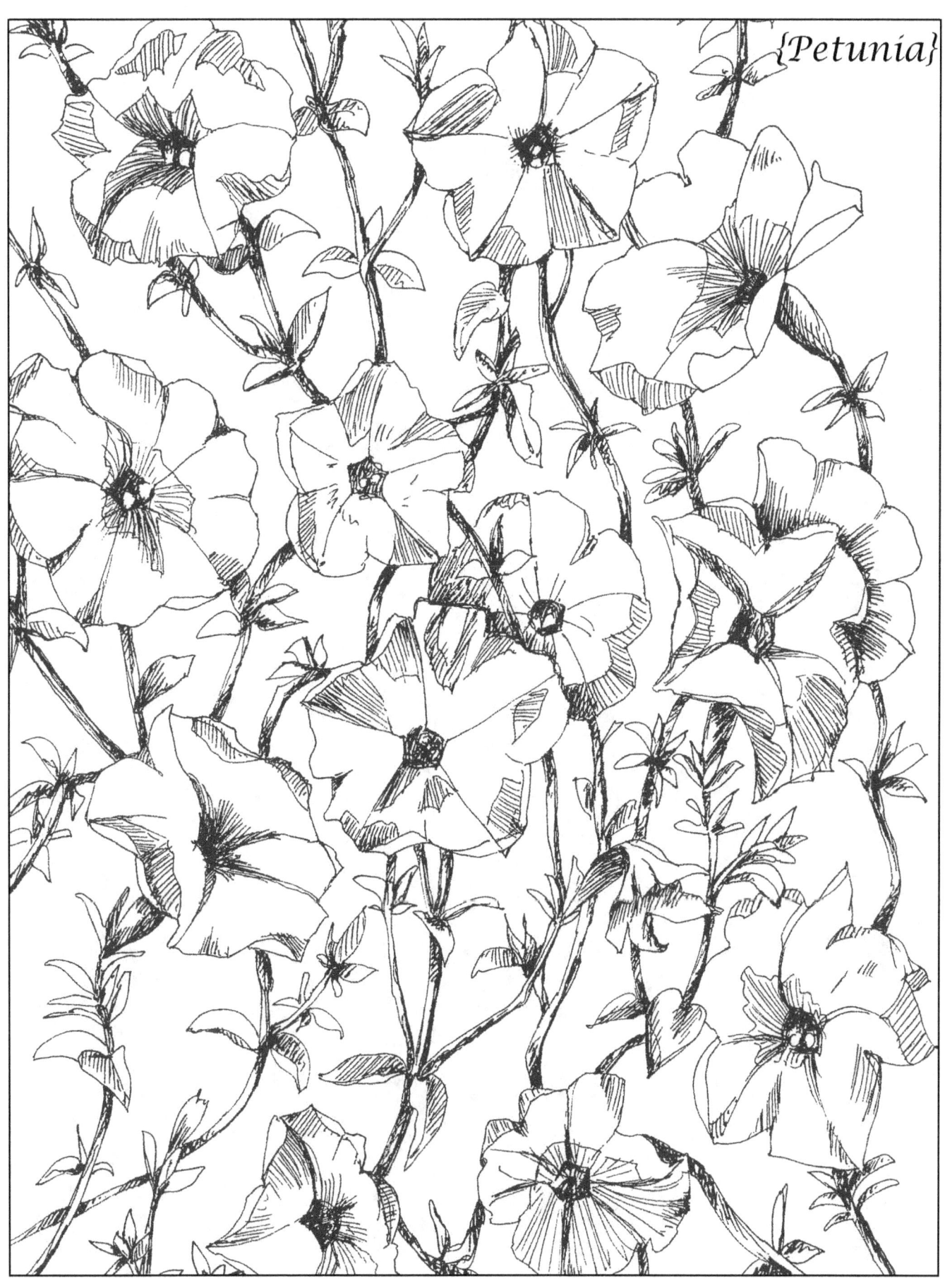

{Petunia}

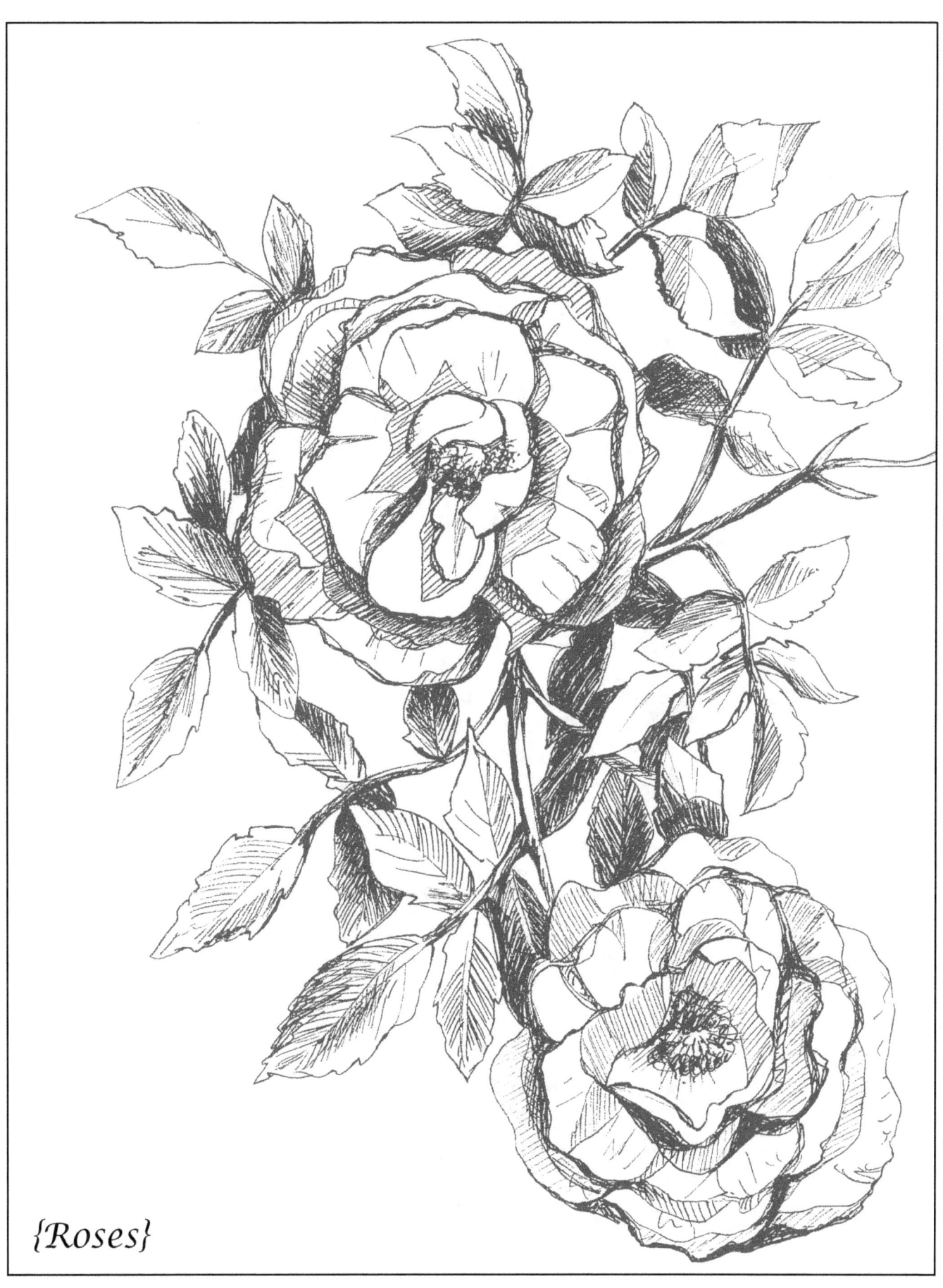

{Roses}

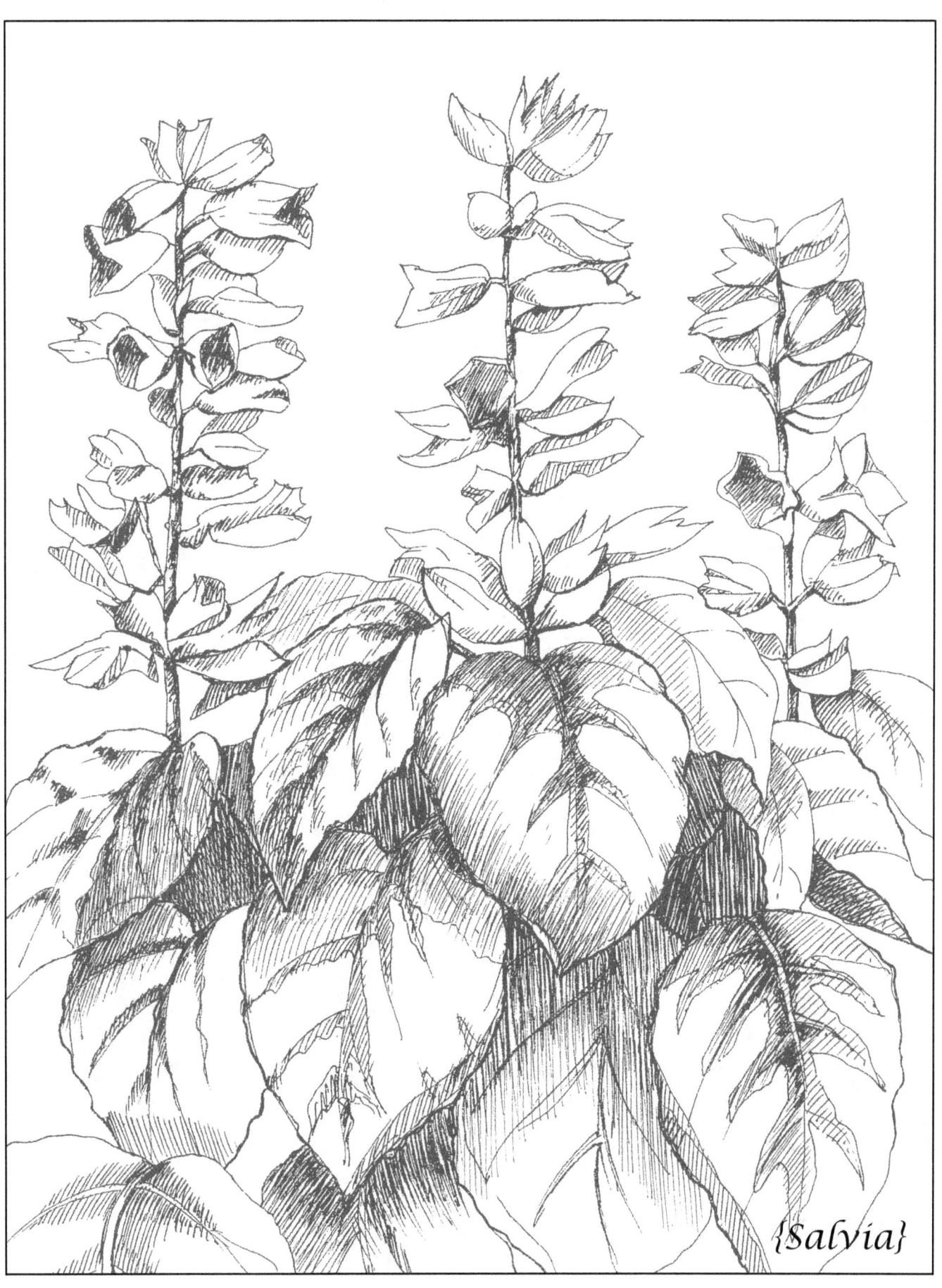

{Salvia}

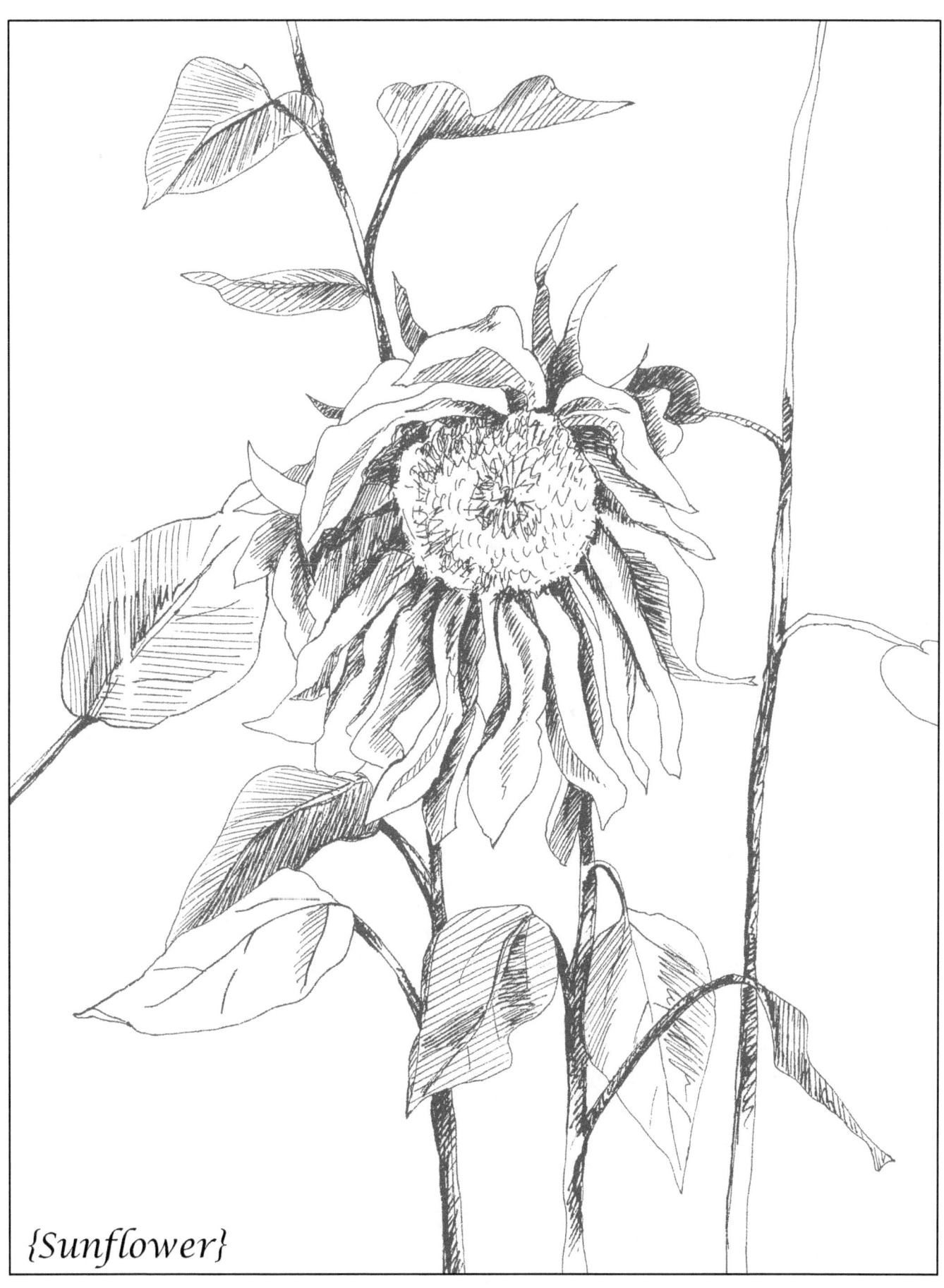

{Sunflower}

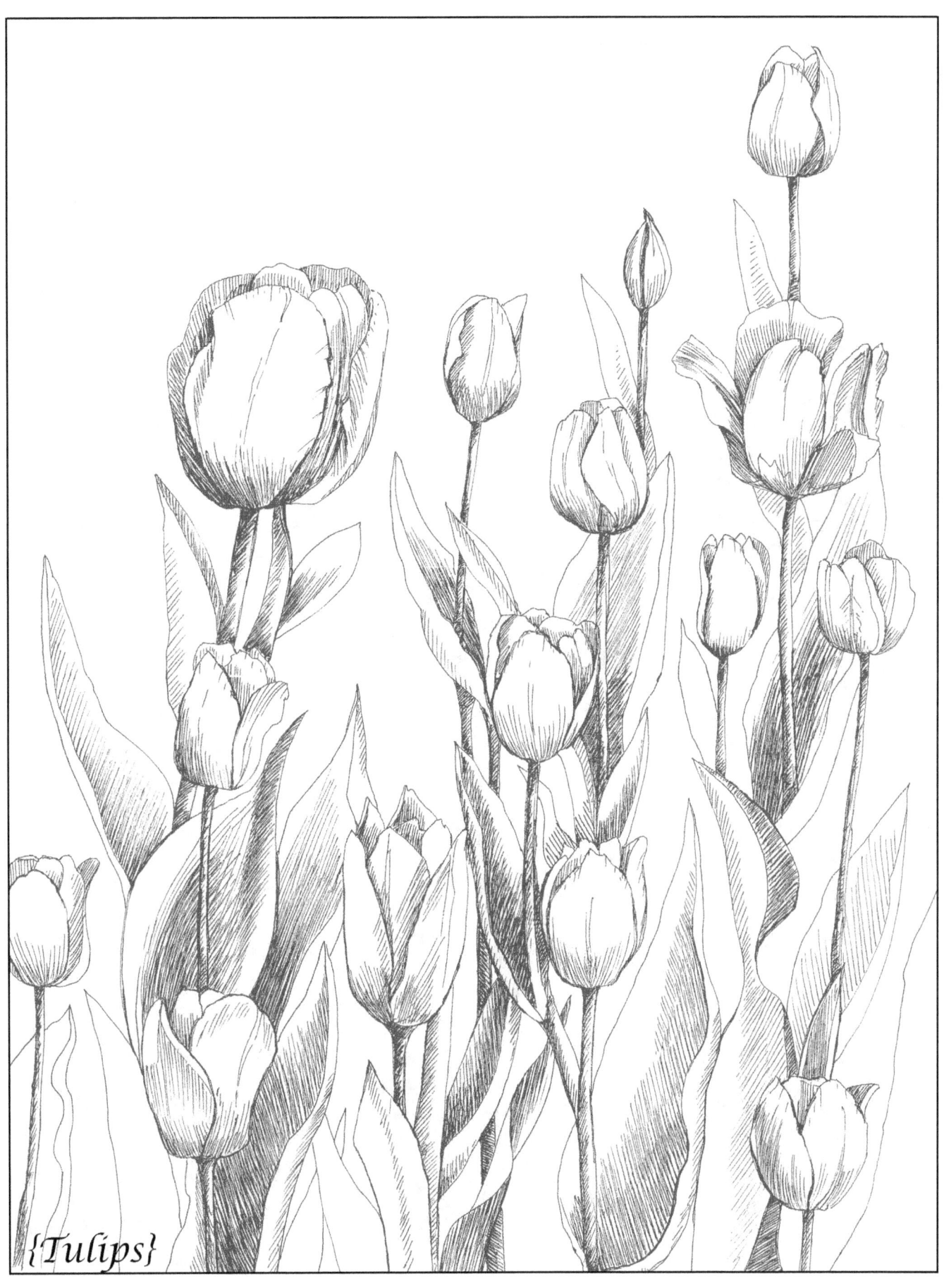

{Tulips}

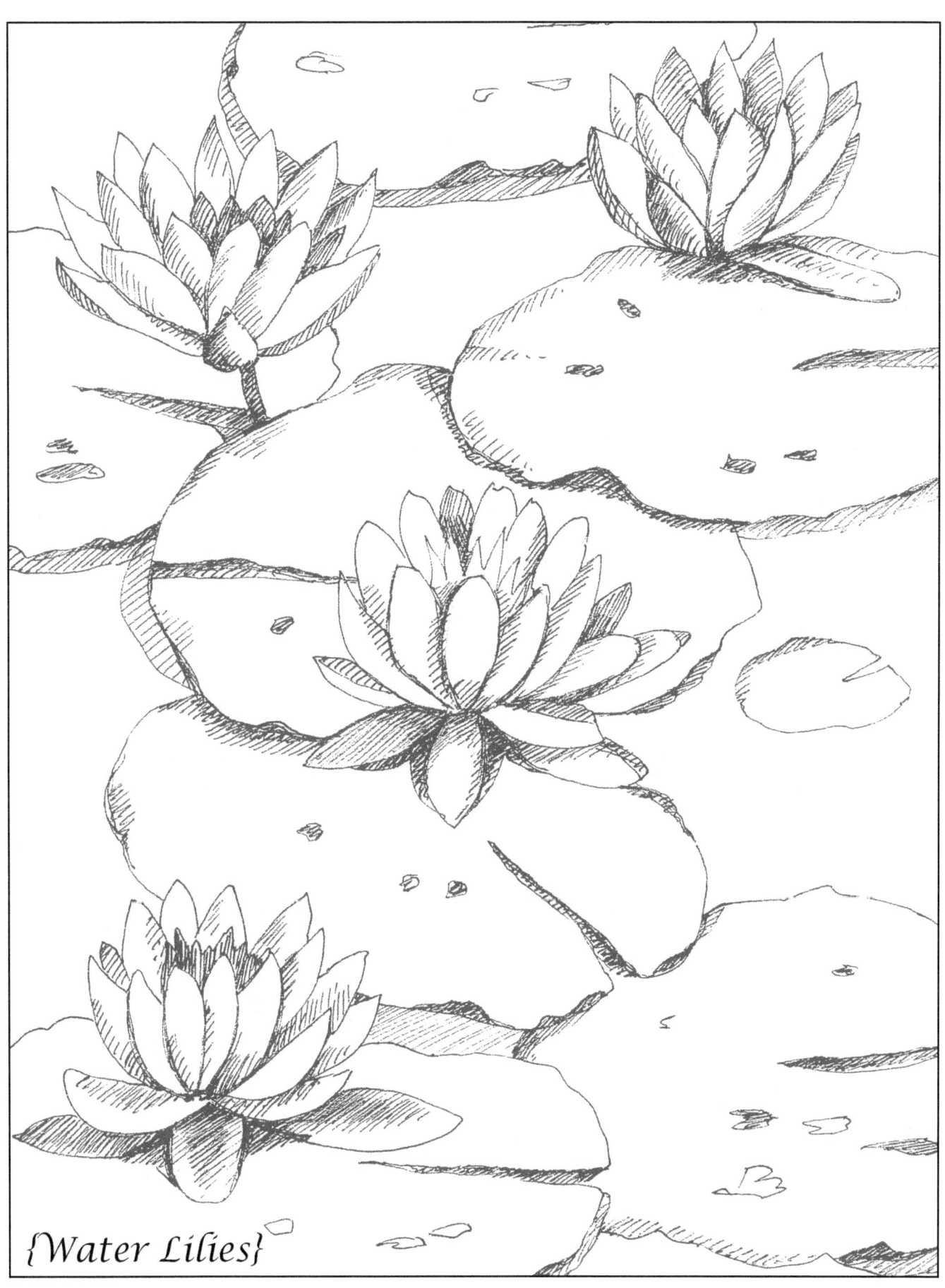

{Water Lilies}

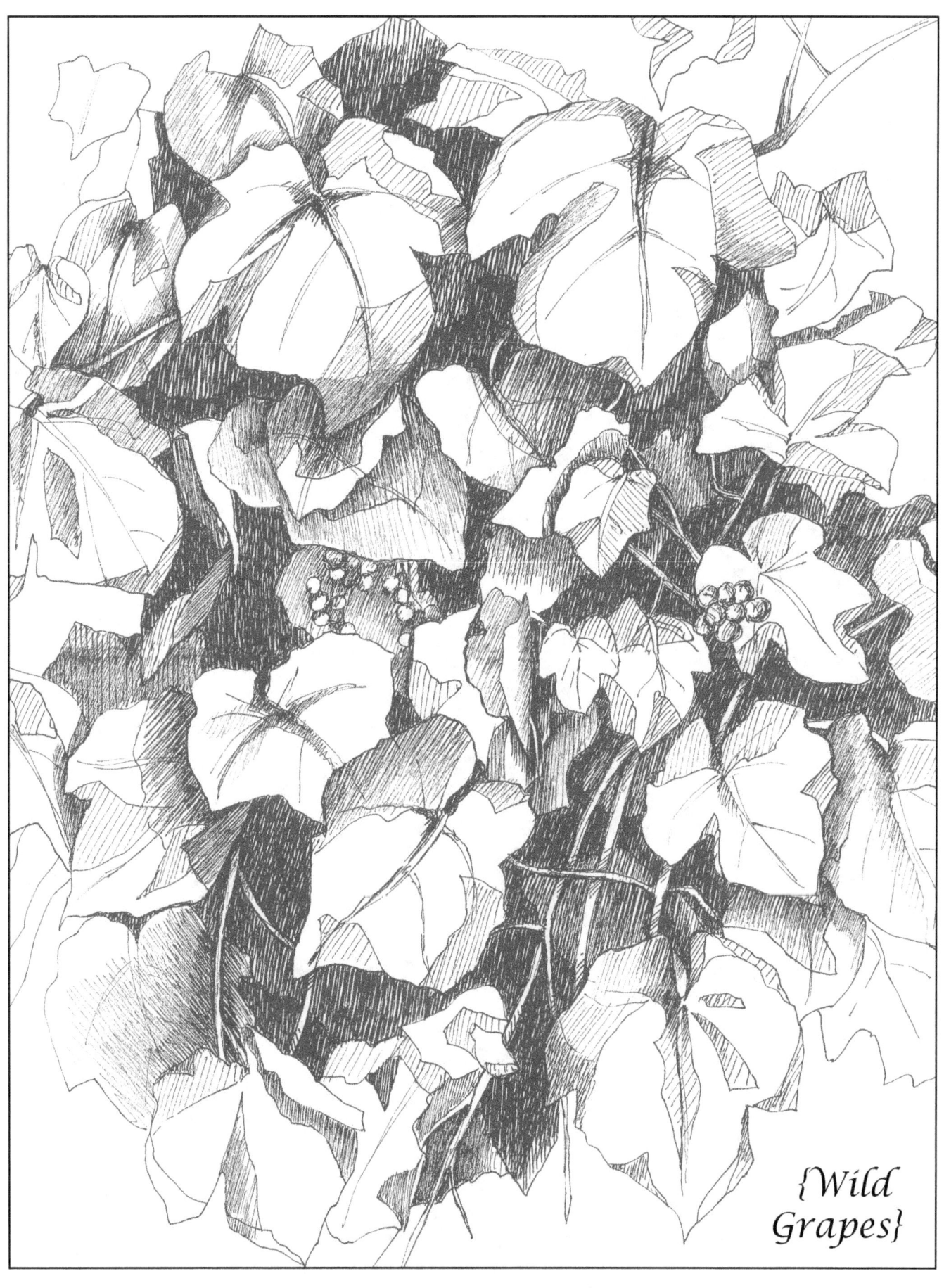

{Wild
Grapes}

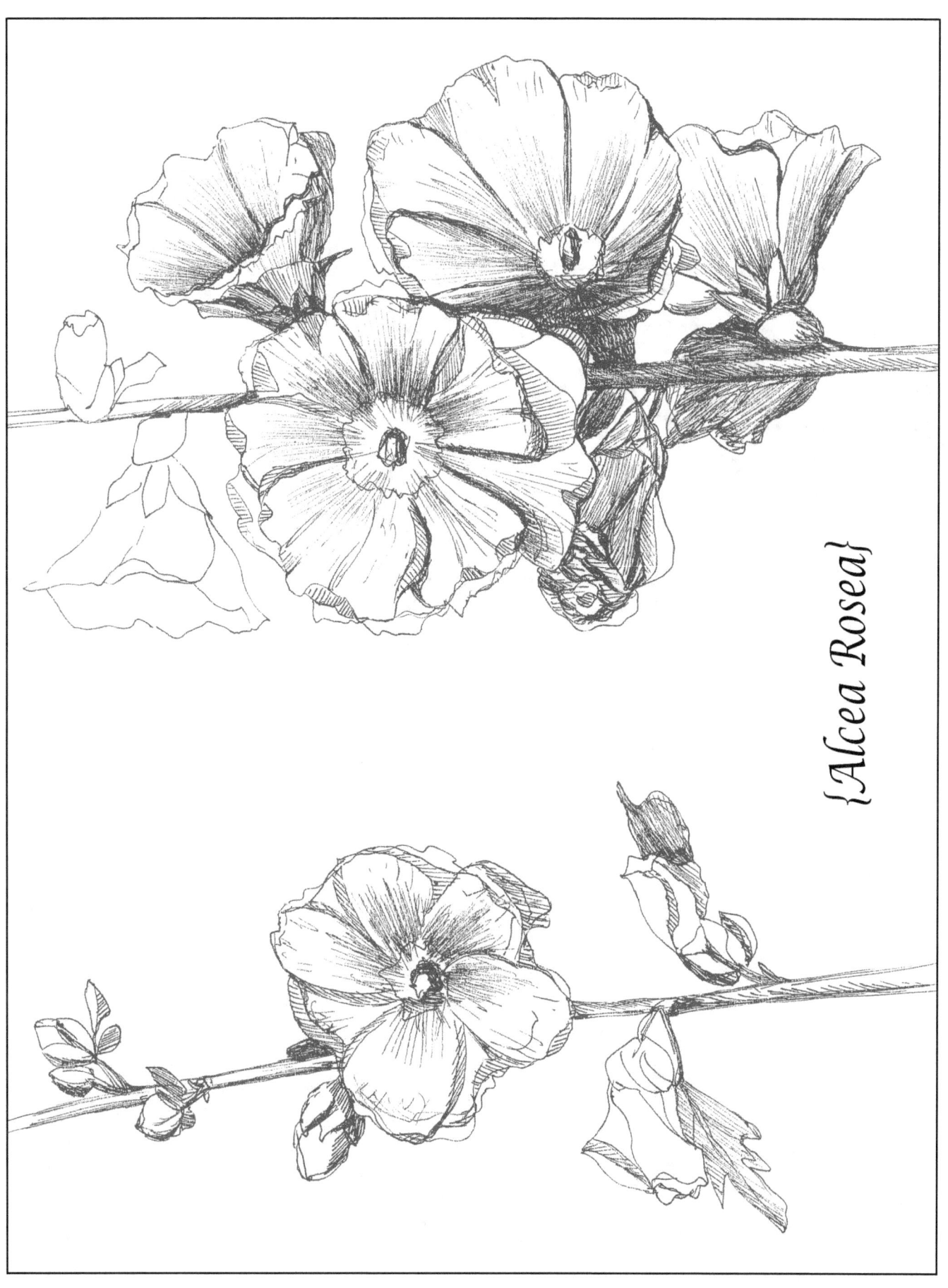

{Alcea Rosea}

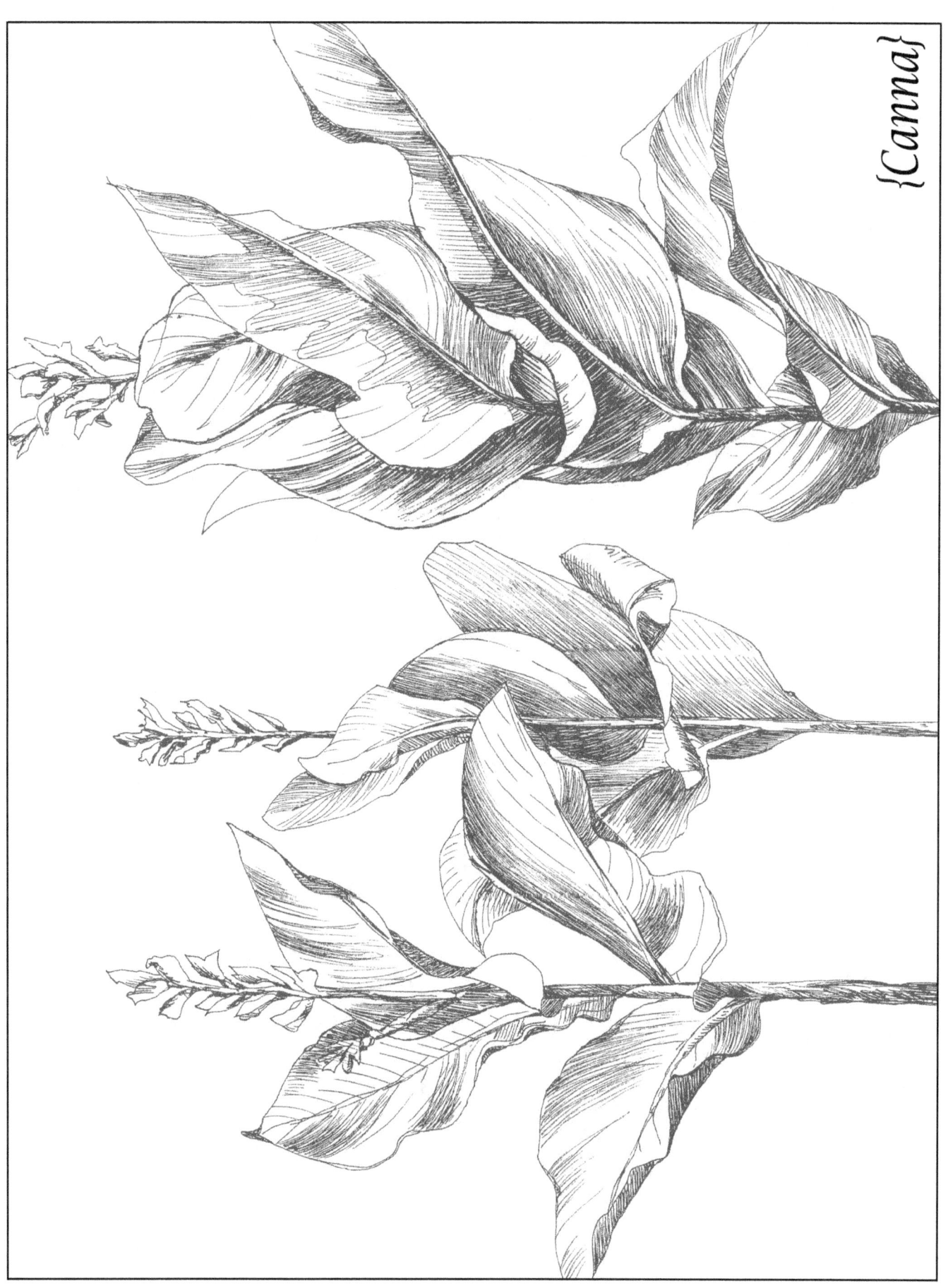

{Canna}

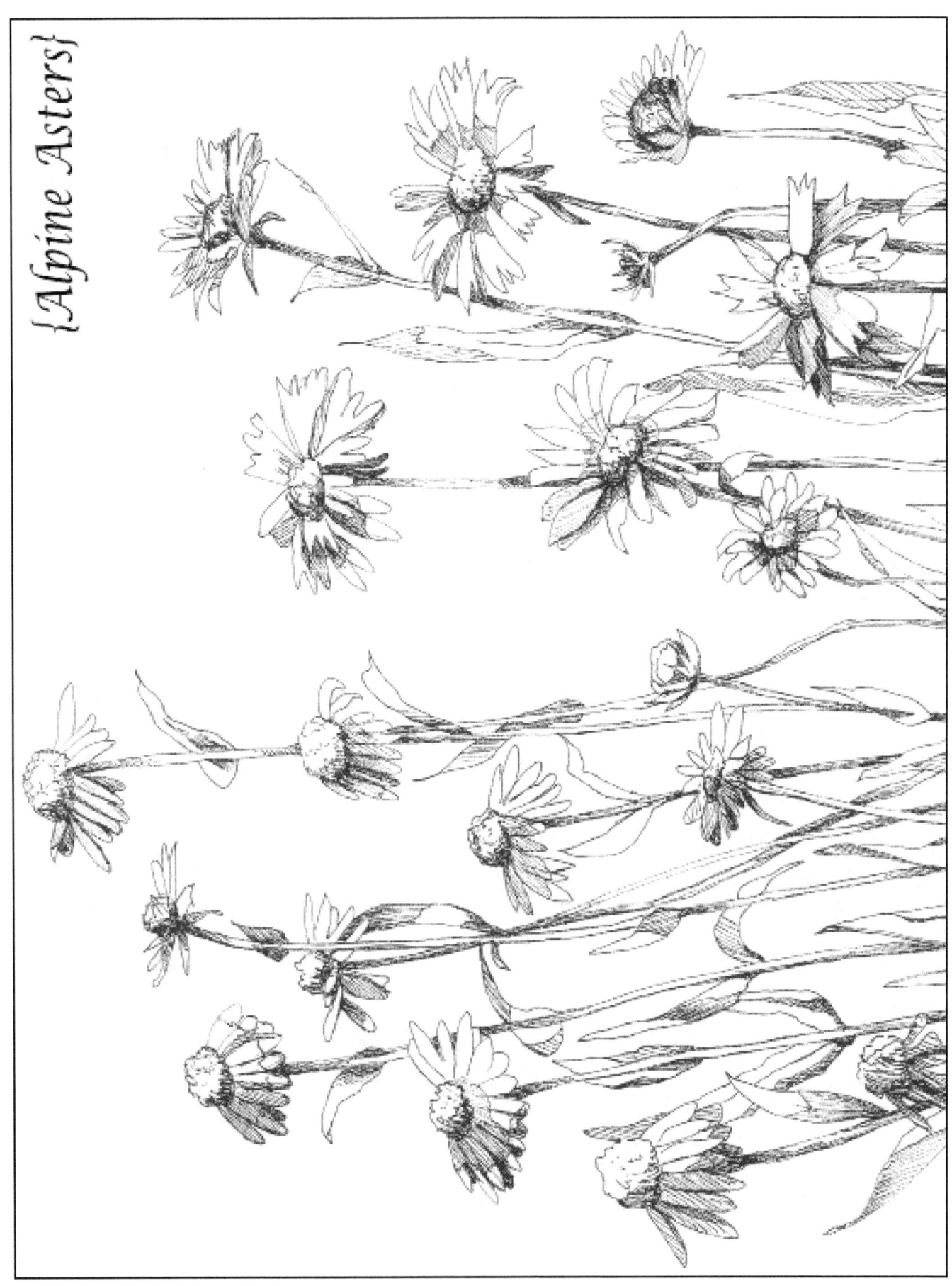

{Alpine Asters}

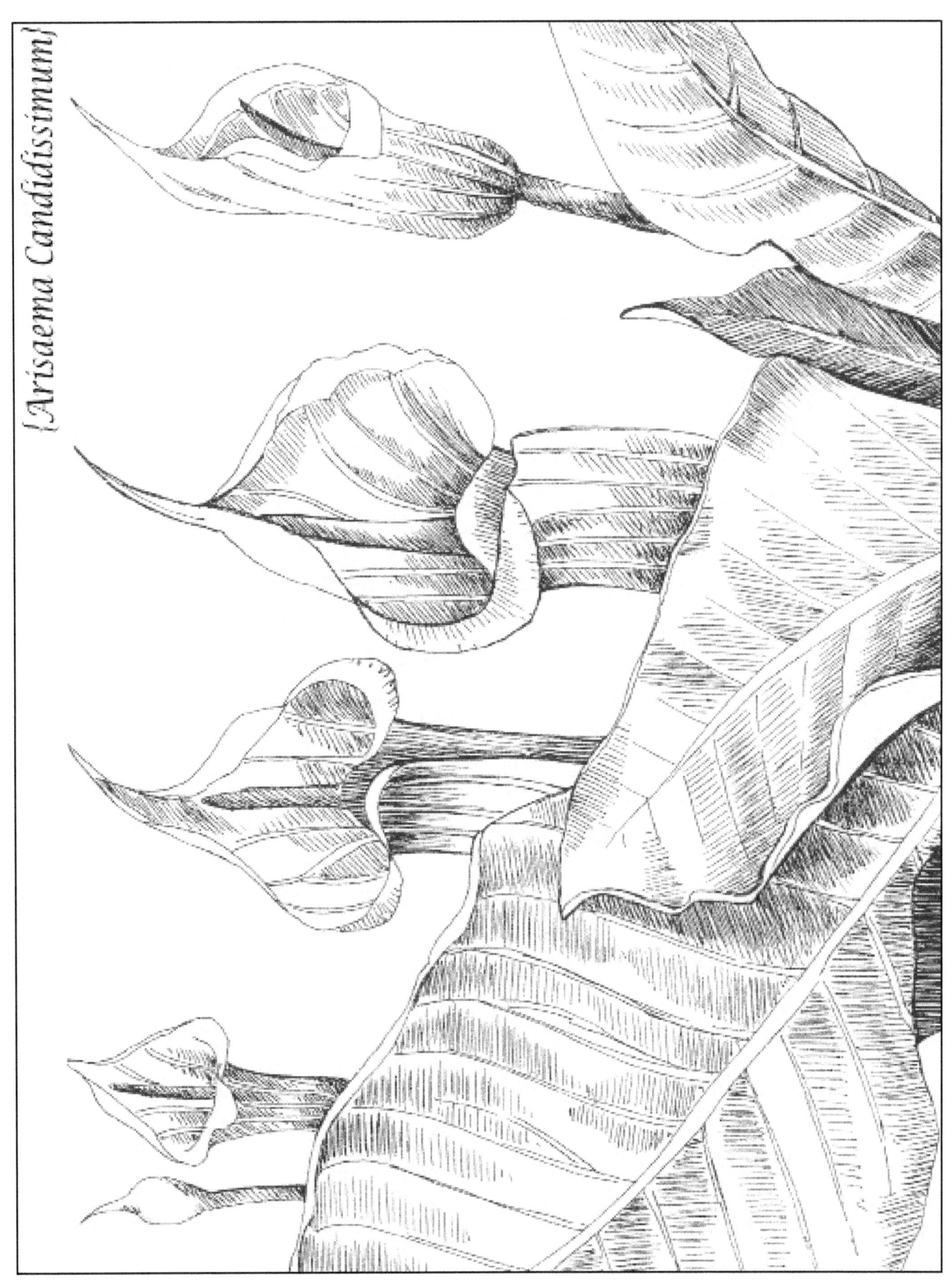

{Arisaema Candidissimum}

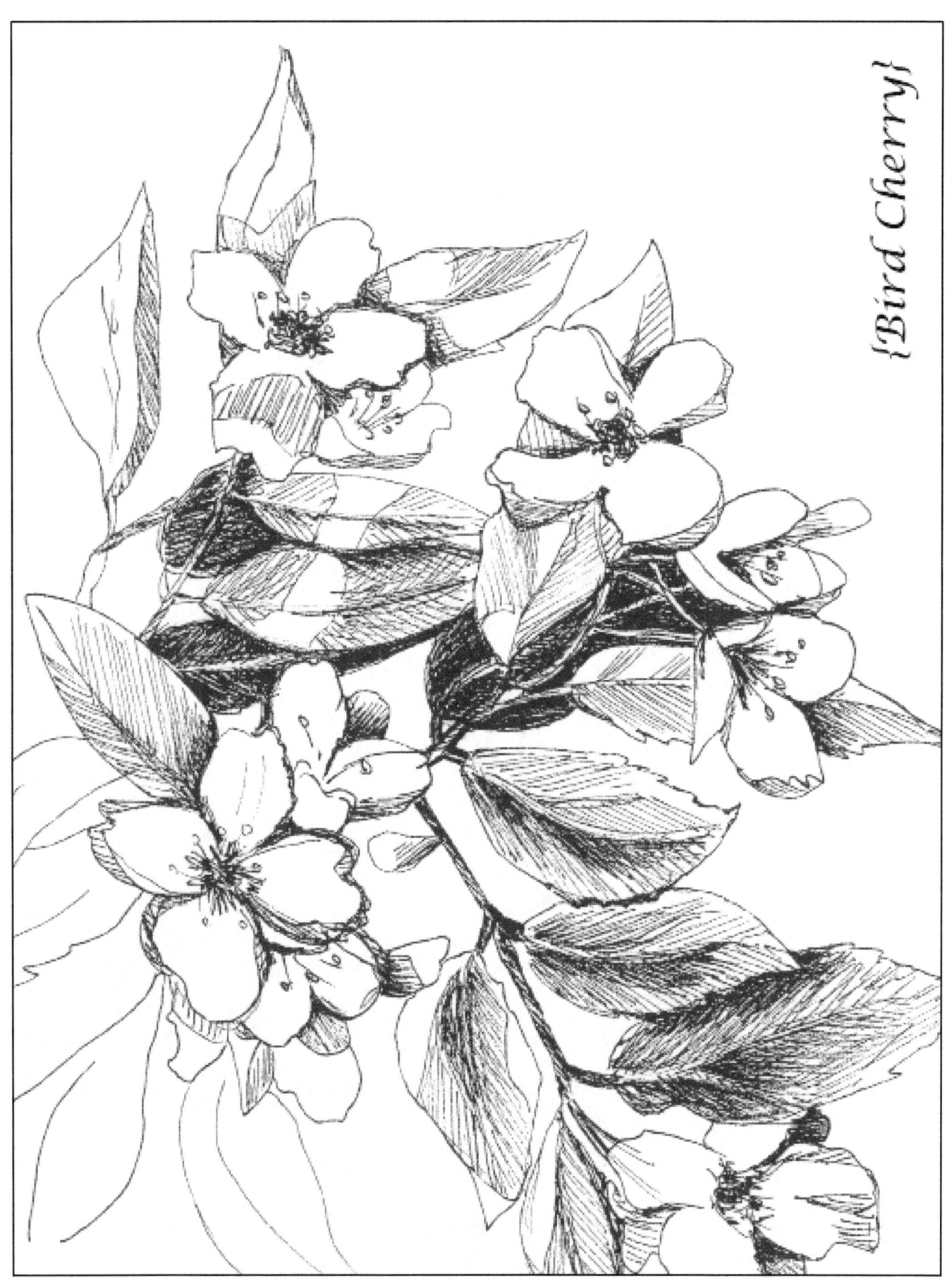

¡Bird Cherry!

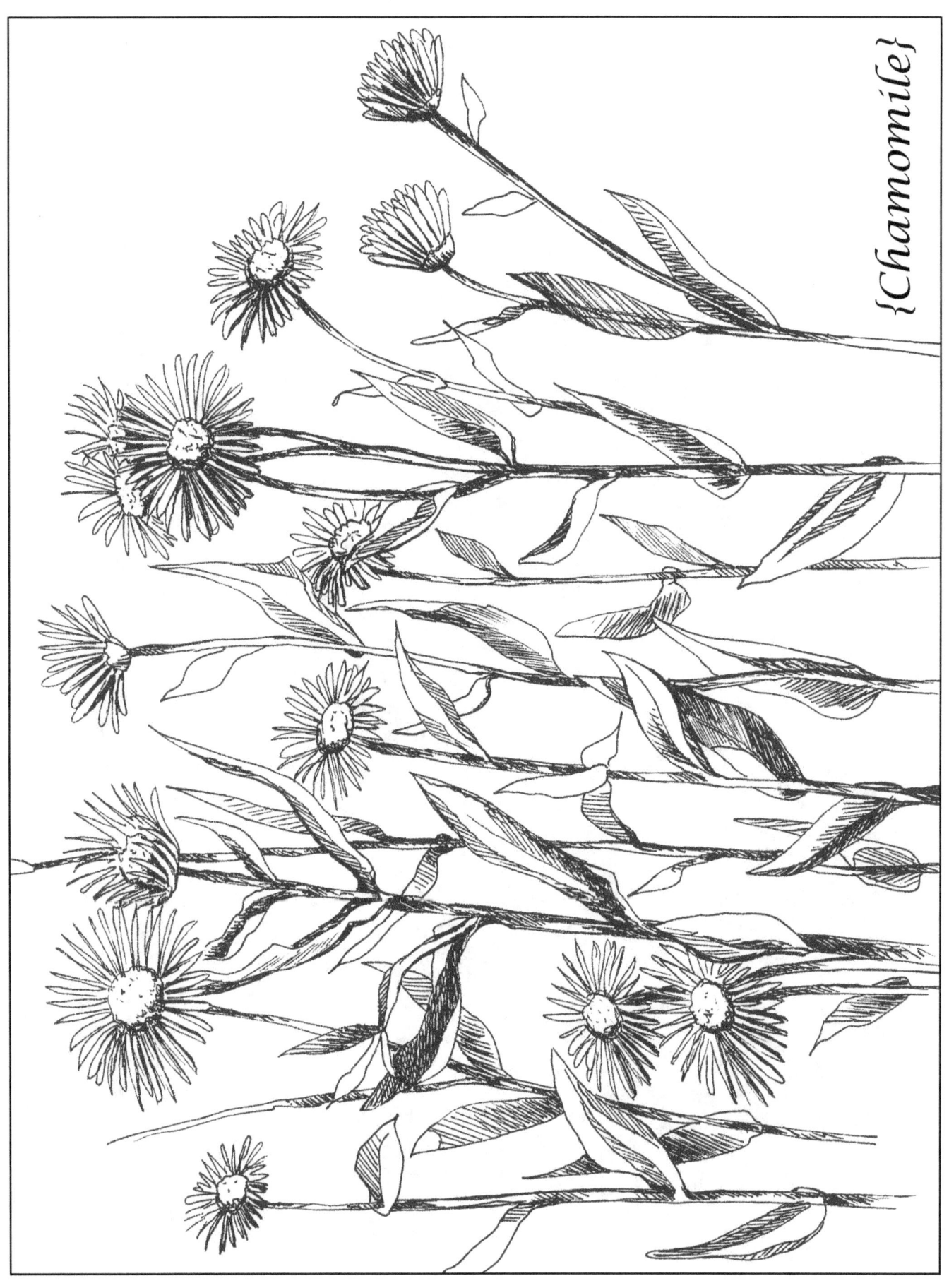

{Chamomile}

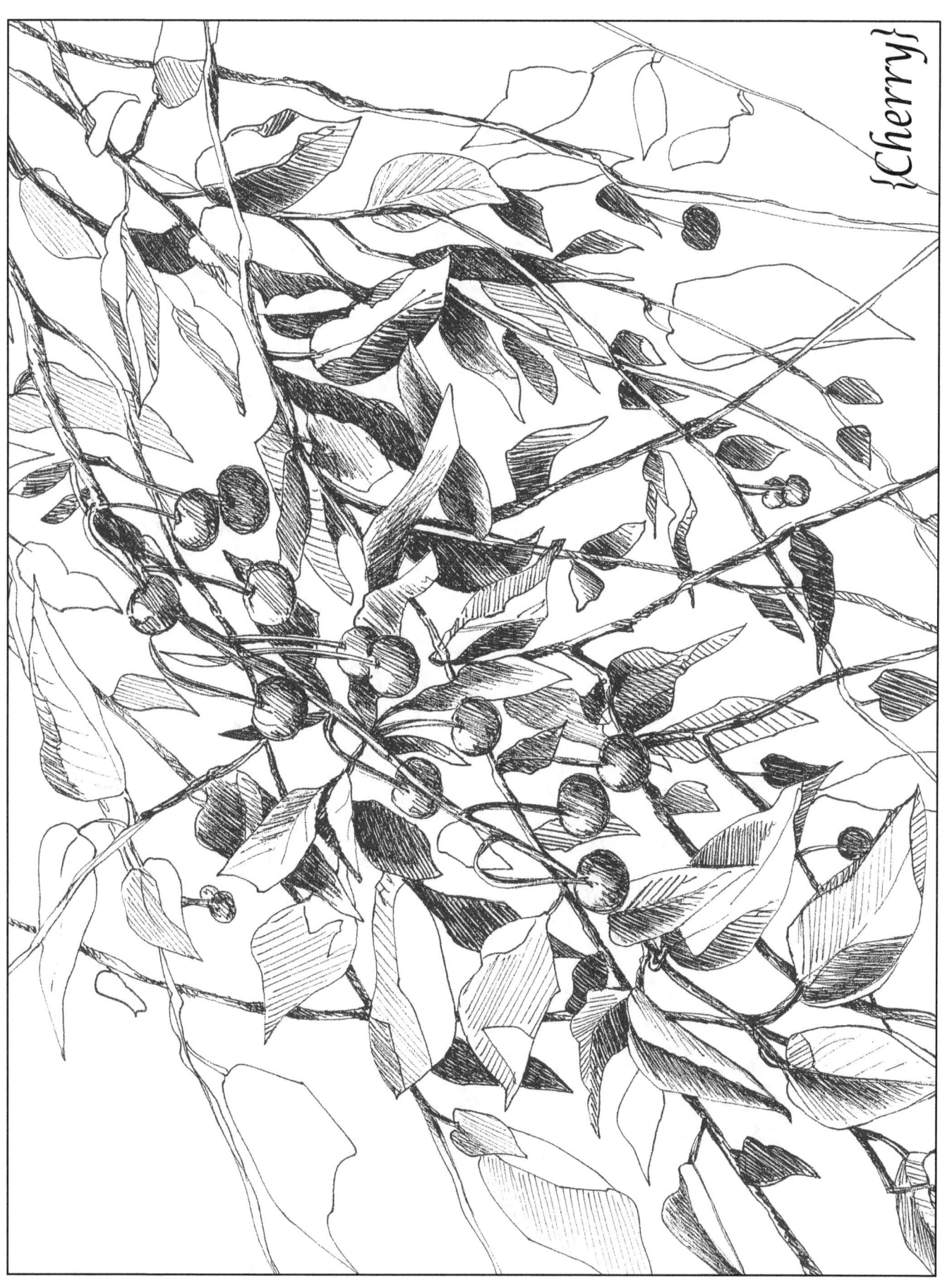

{Cherry}

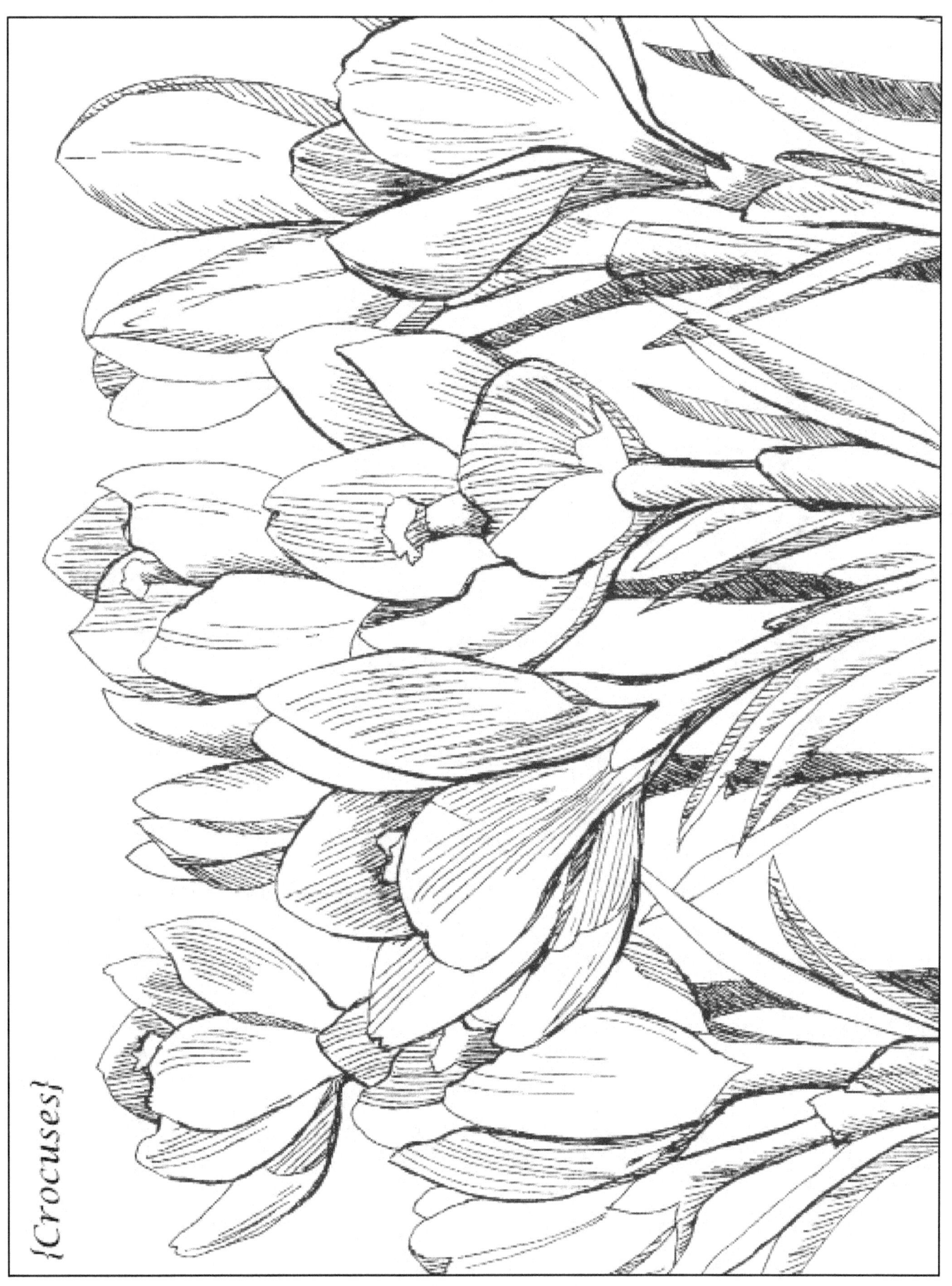

{Crocuses}

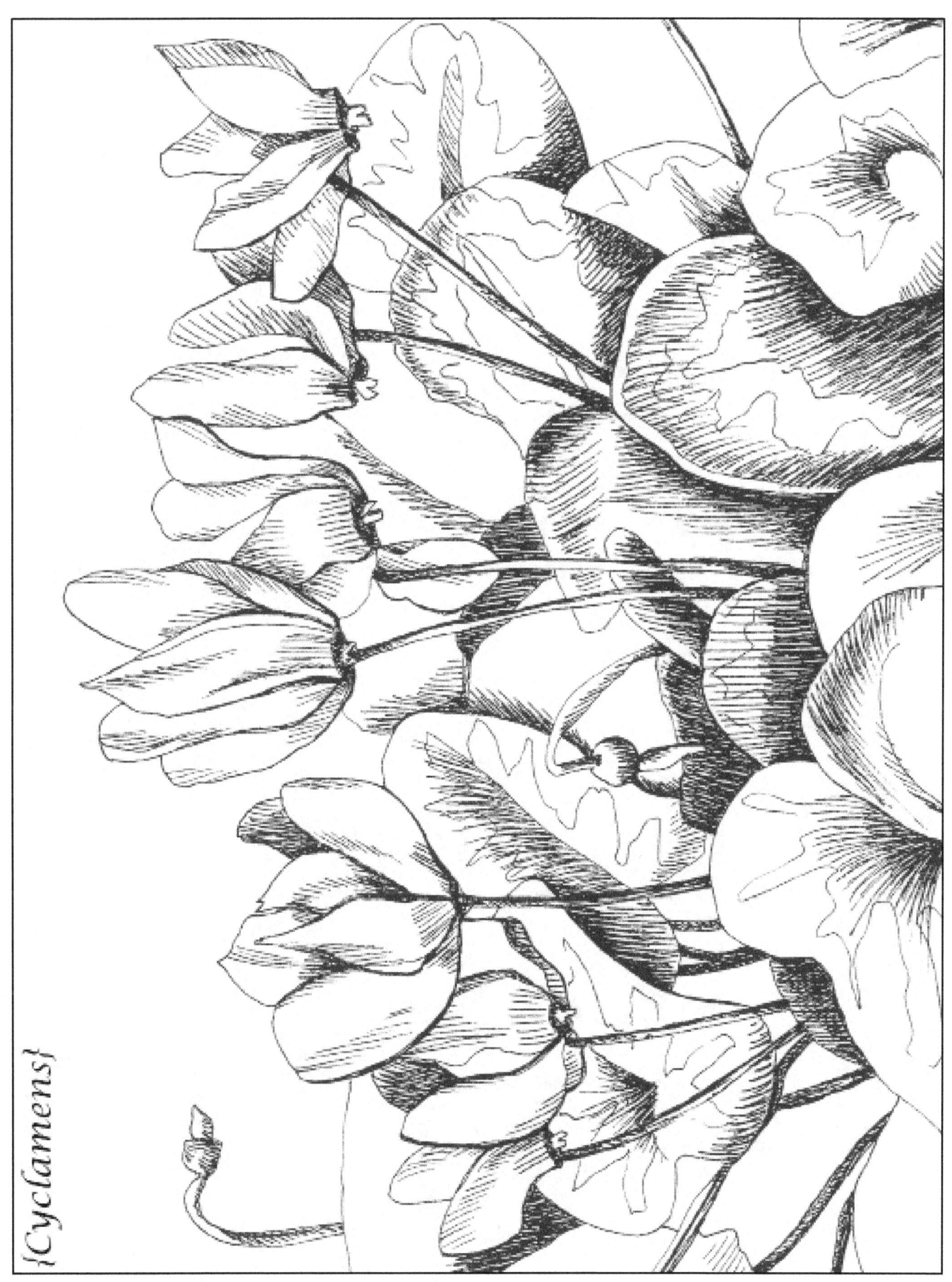

{Cyclamens}

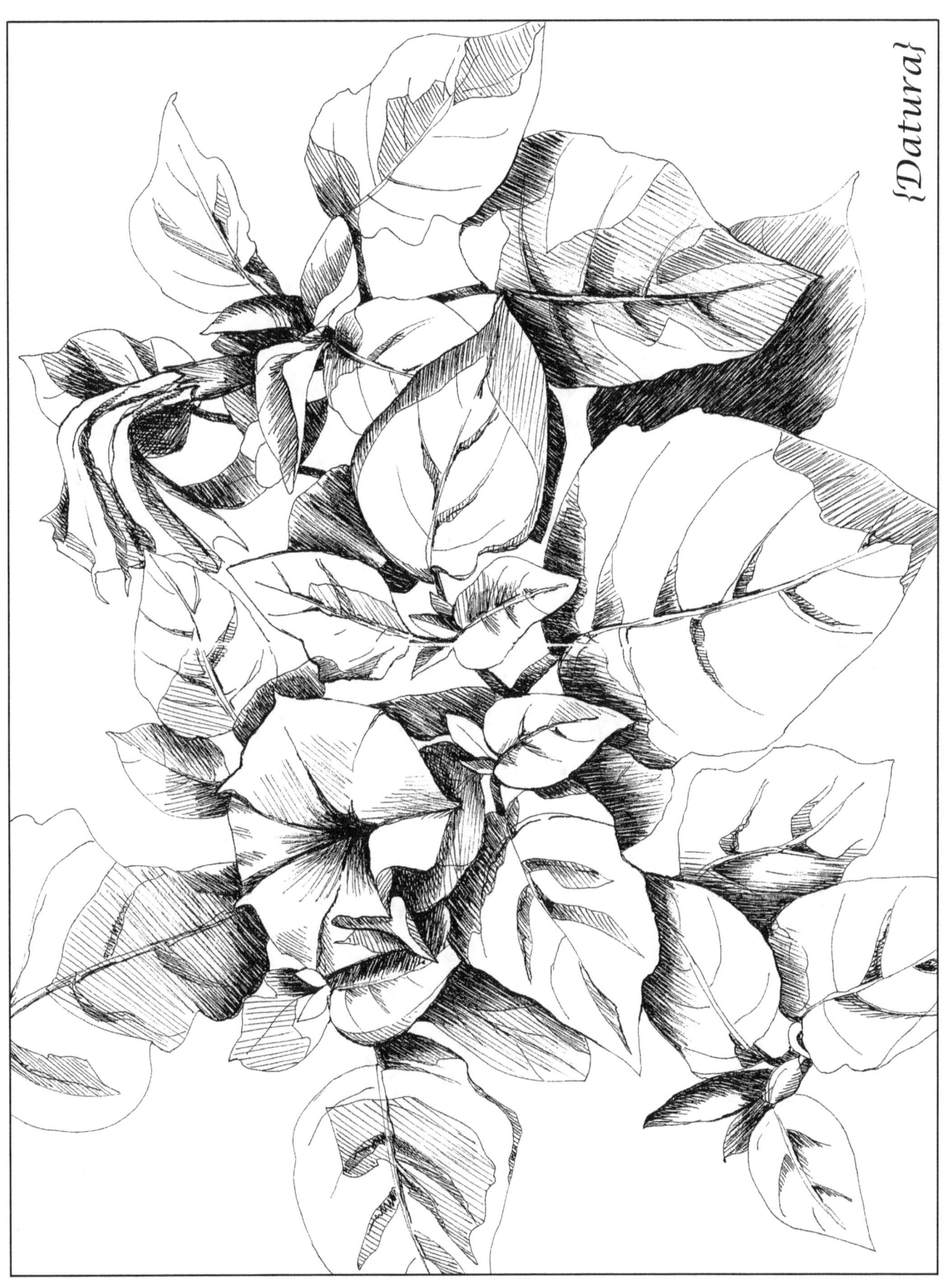

{Datura}

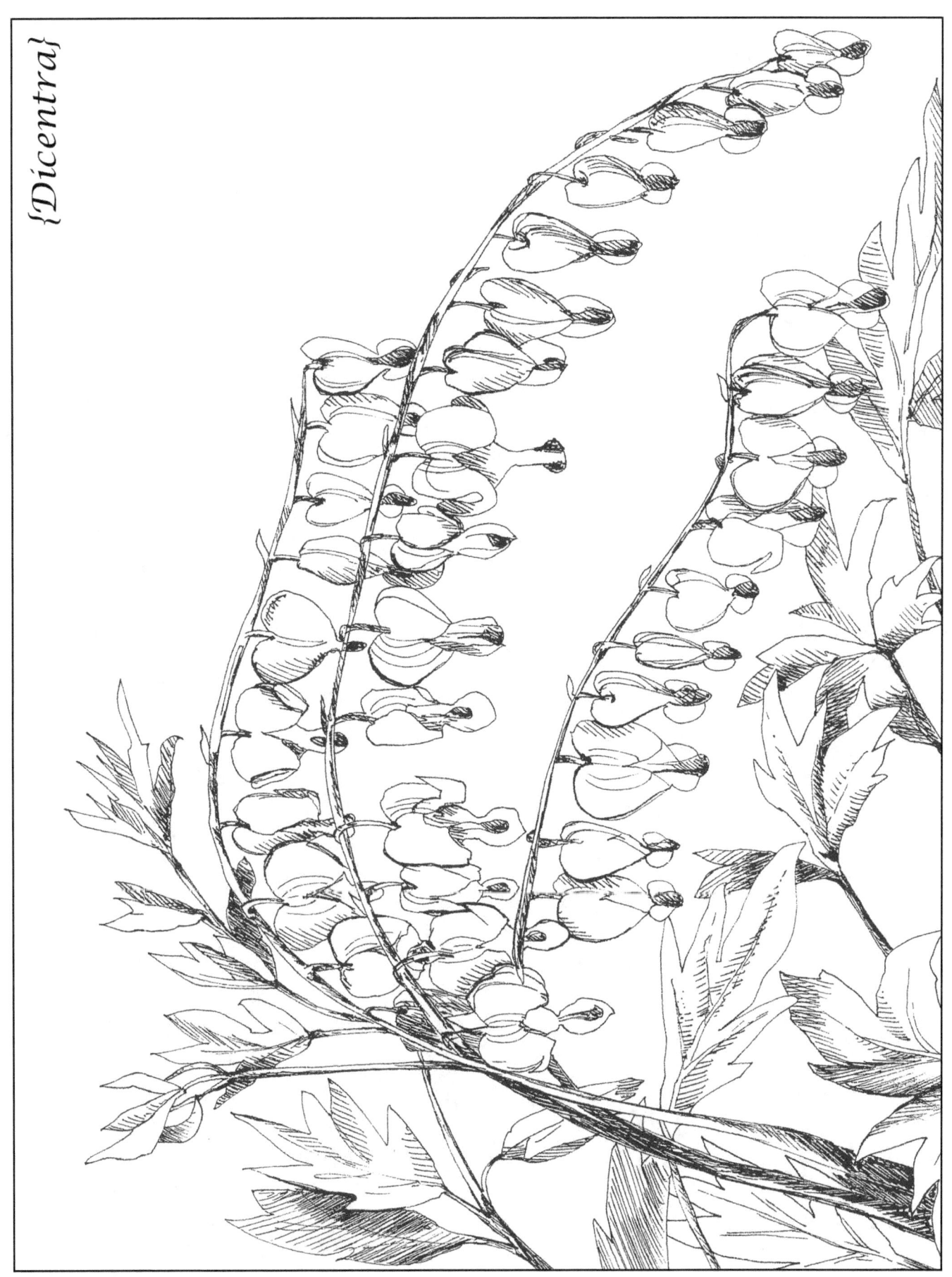

{Dicentra}

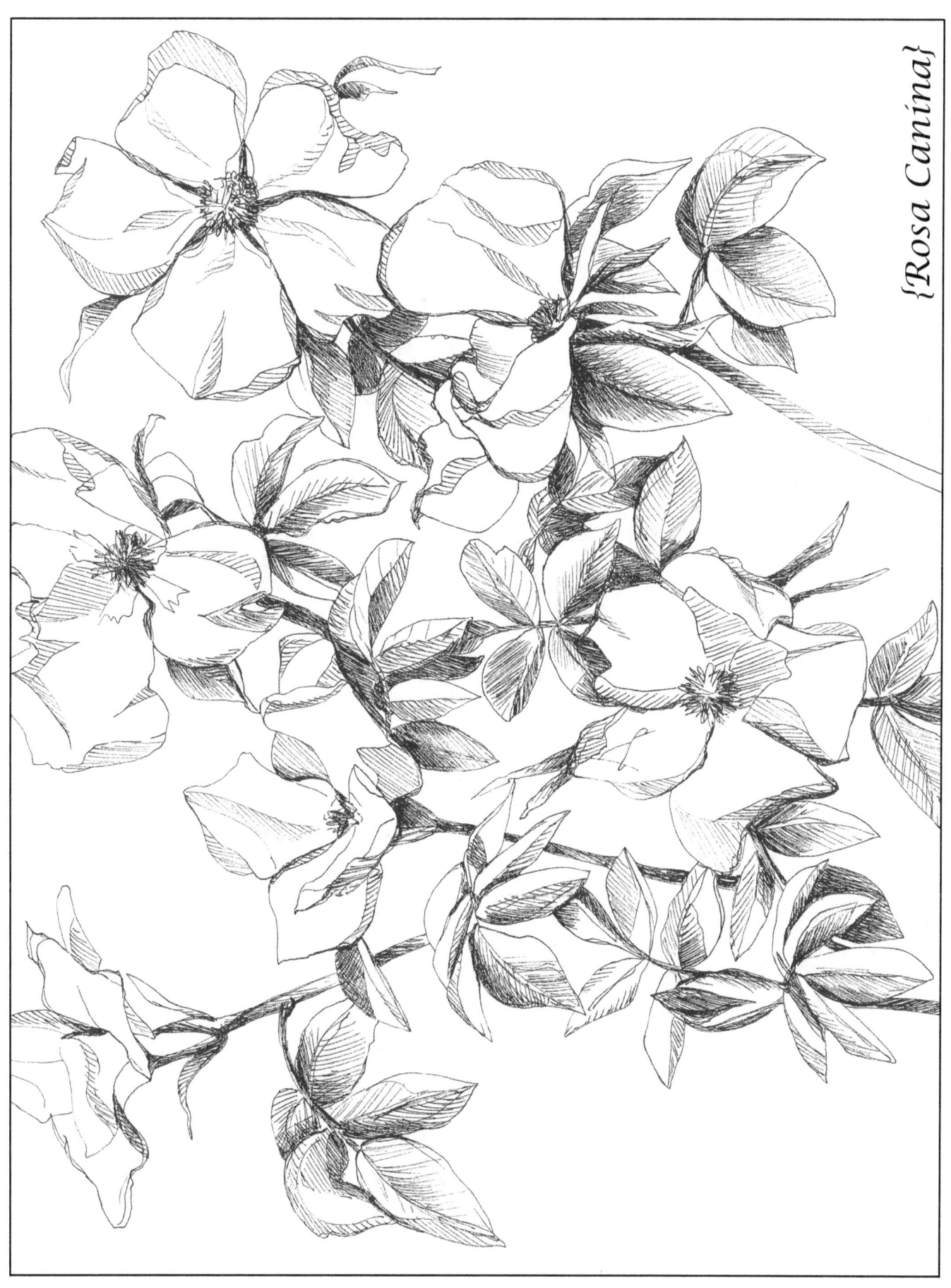

{Rosa Canina}

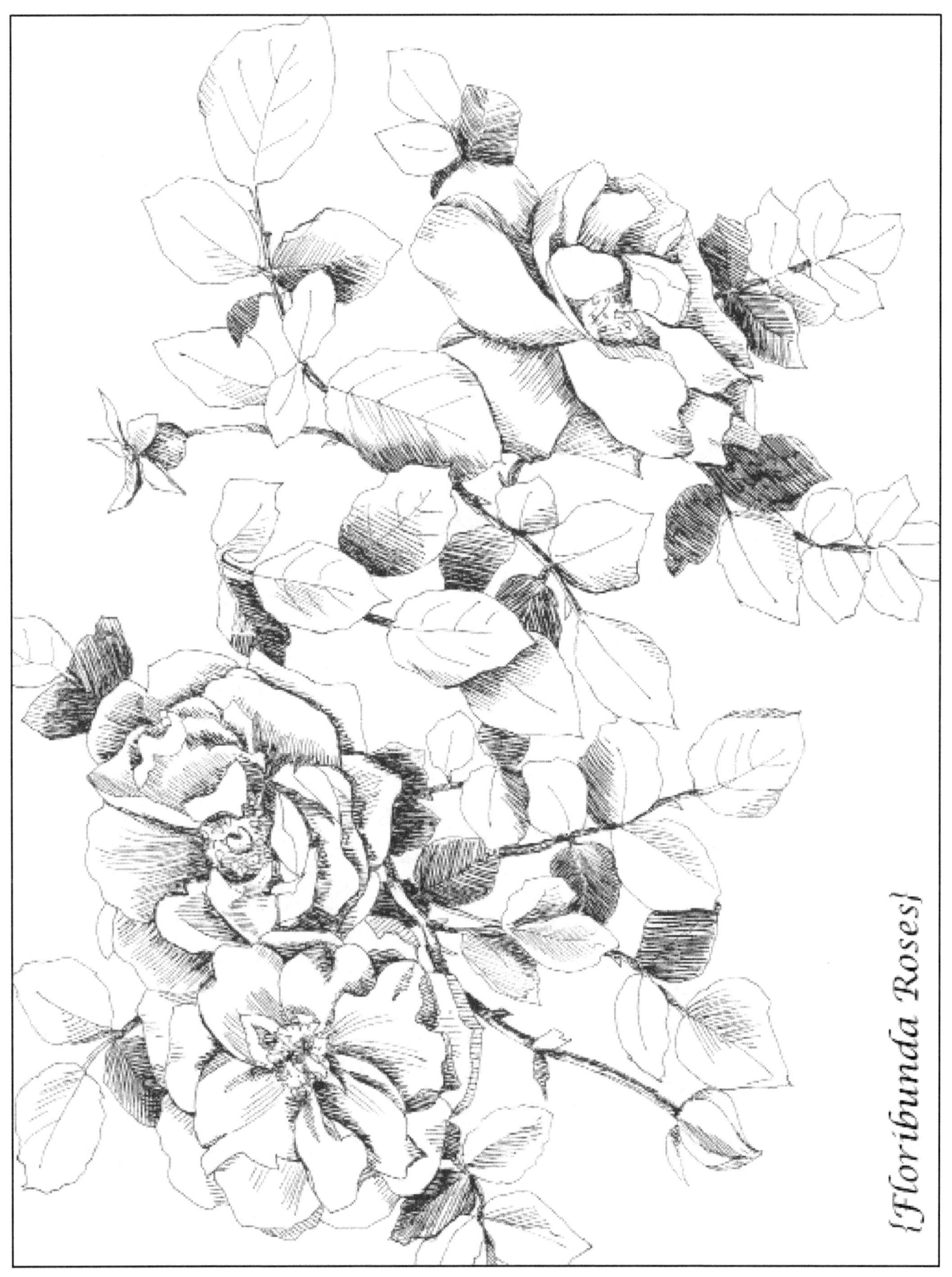

{Floribunda Roses}

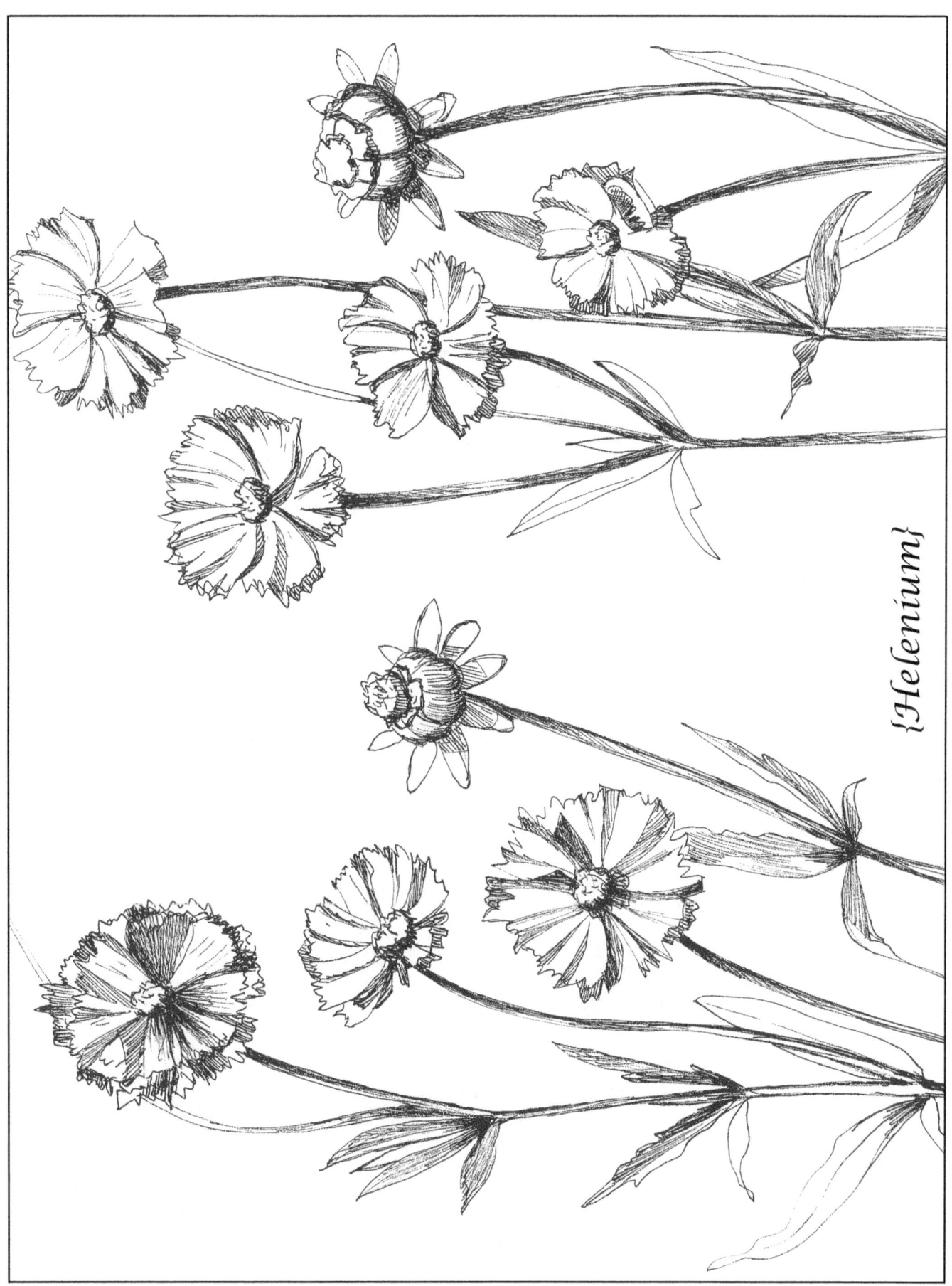

{Helenium}

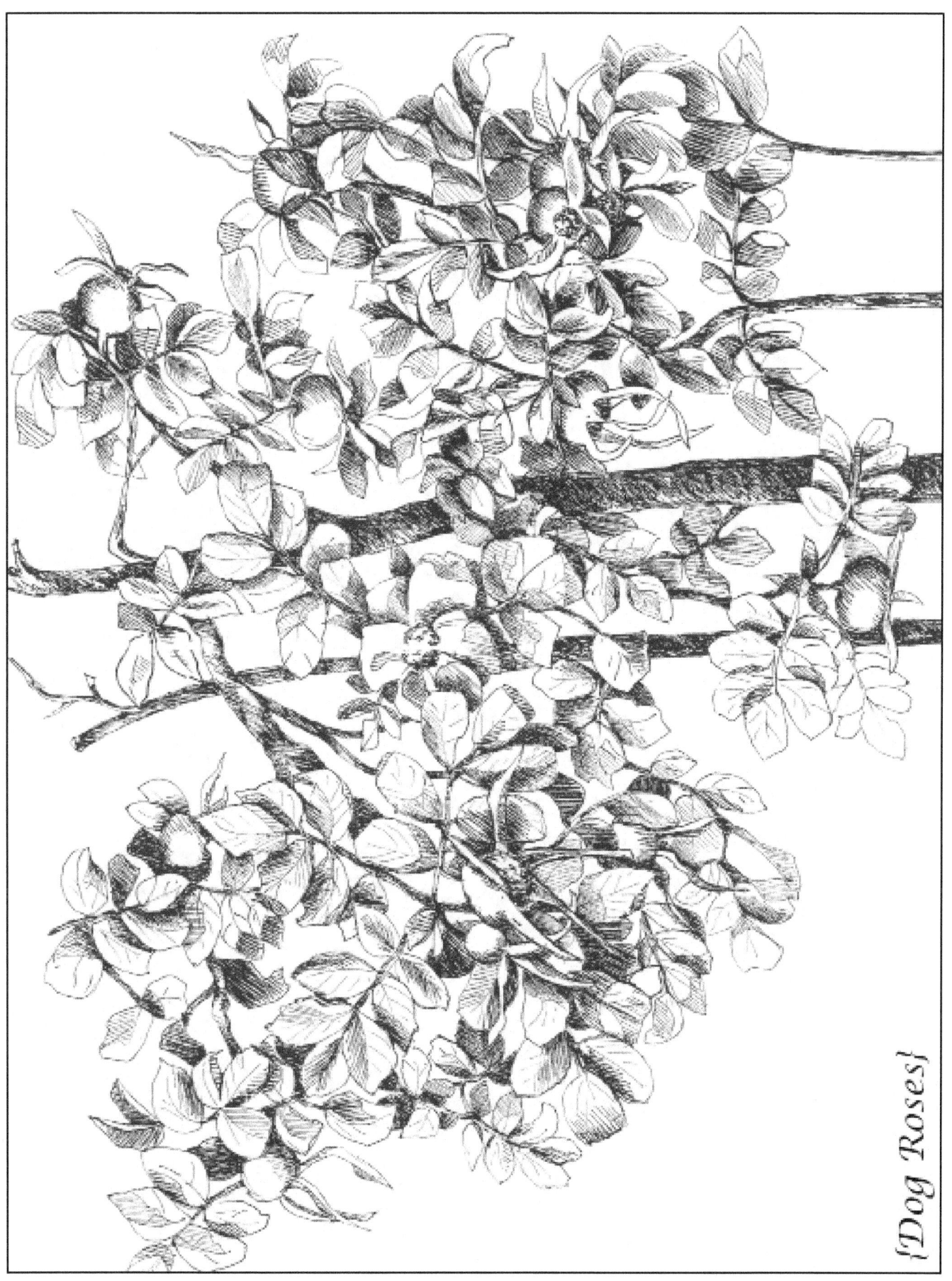

{Dog Roses}

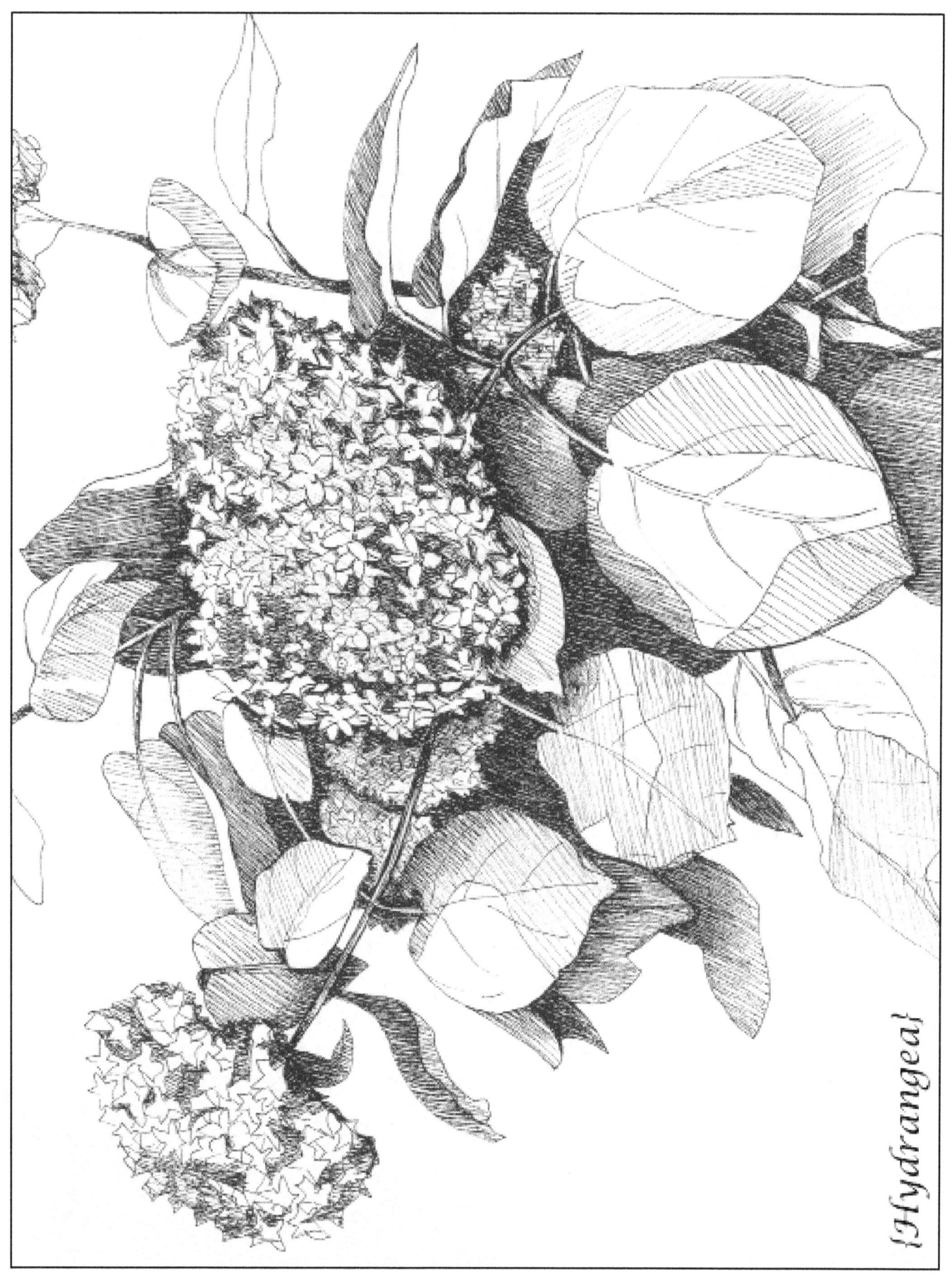

{Hydrangea}

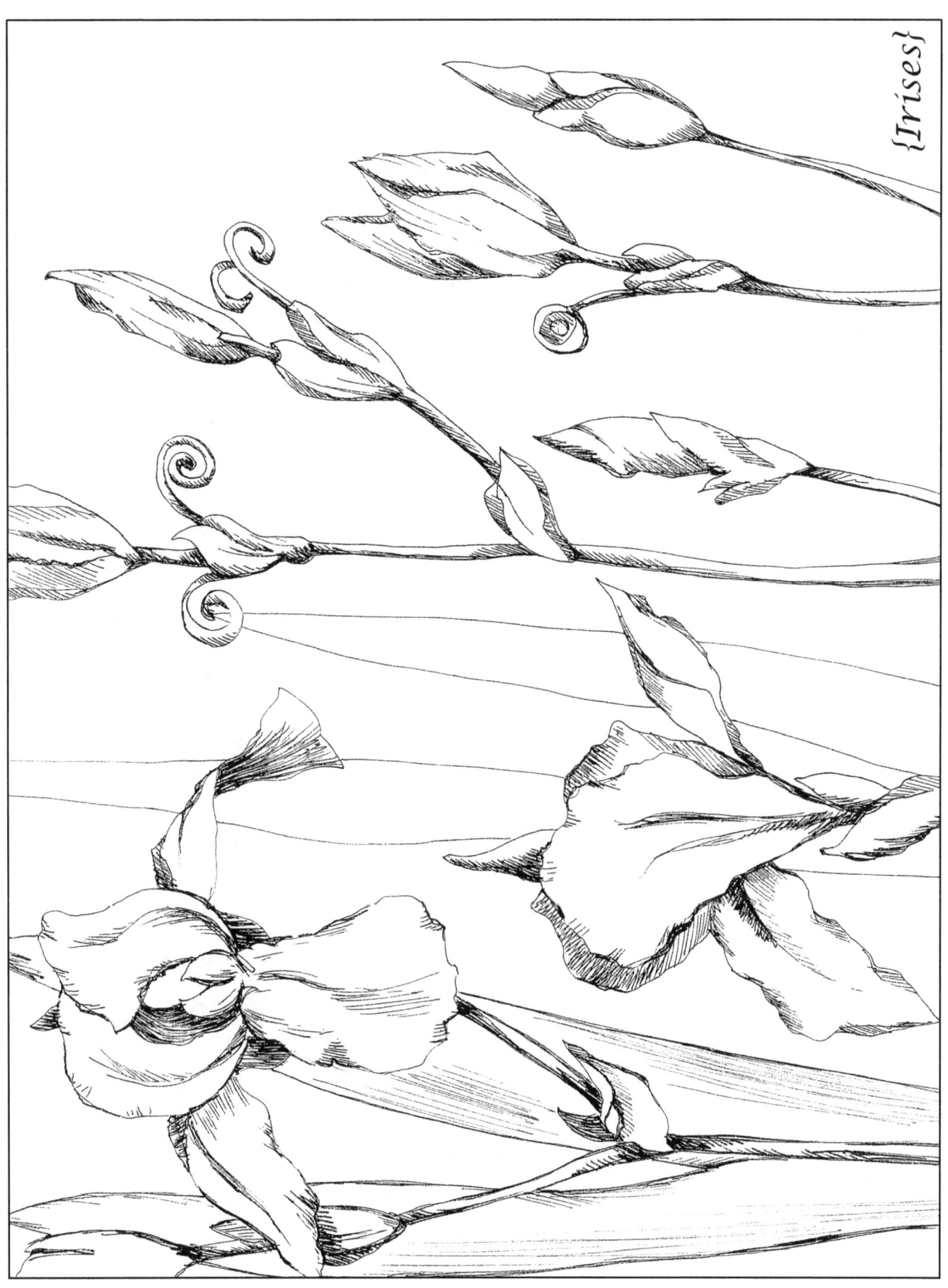

{Irises}

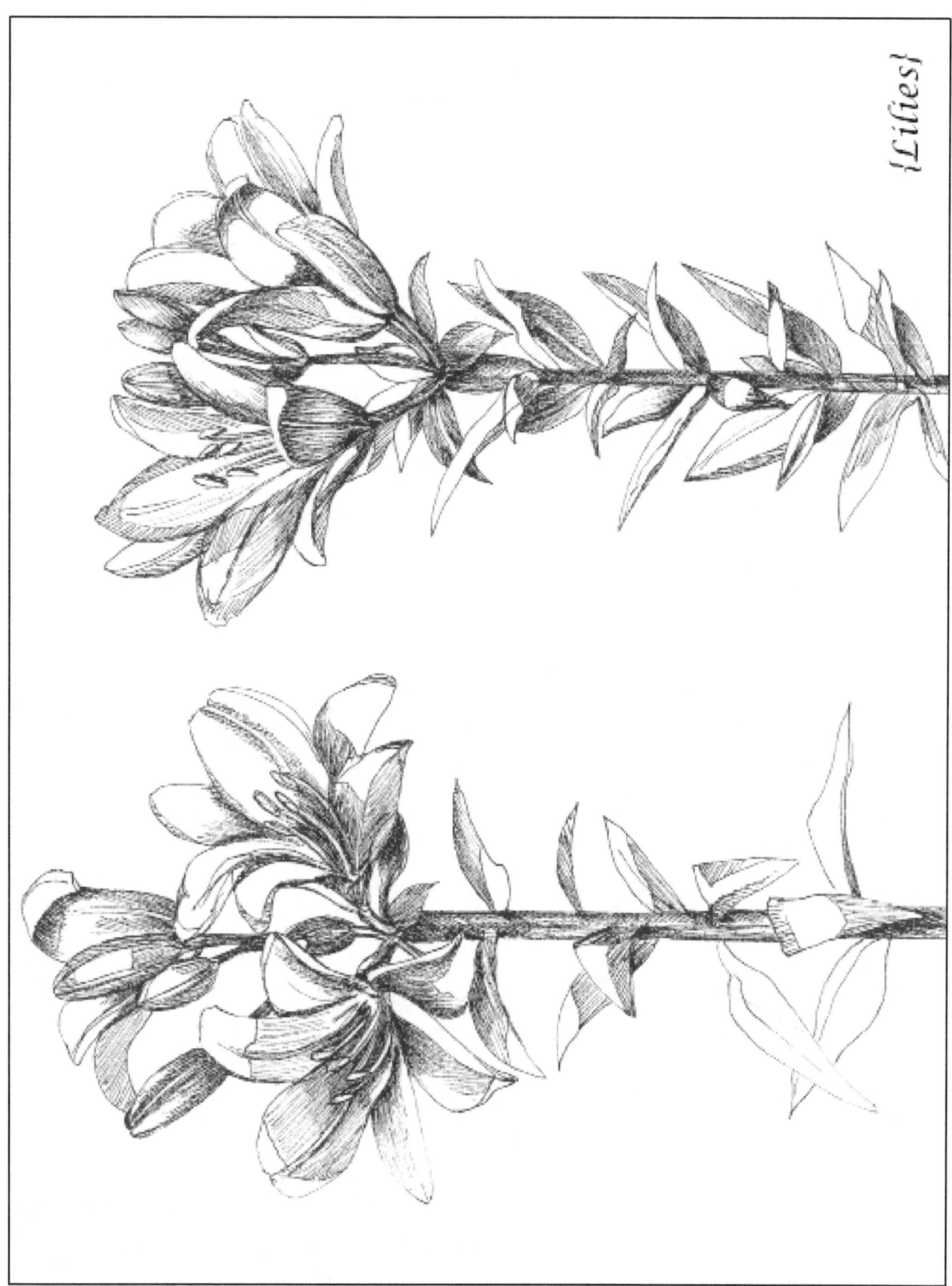

{Lilies}

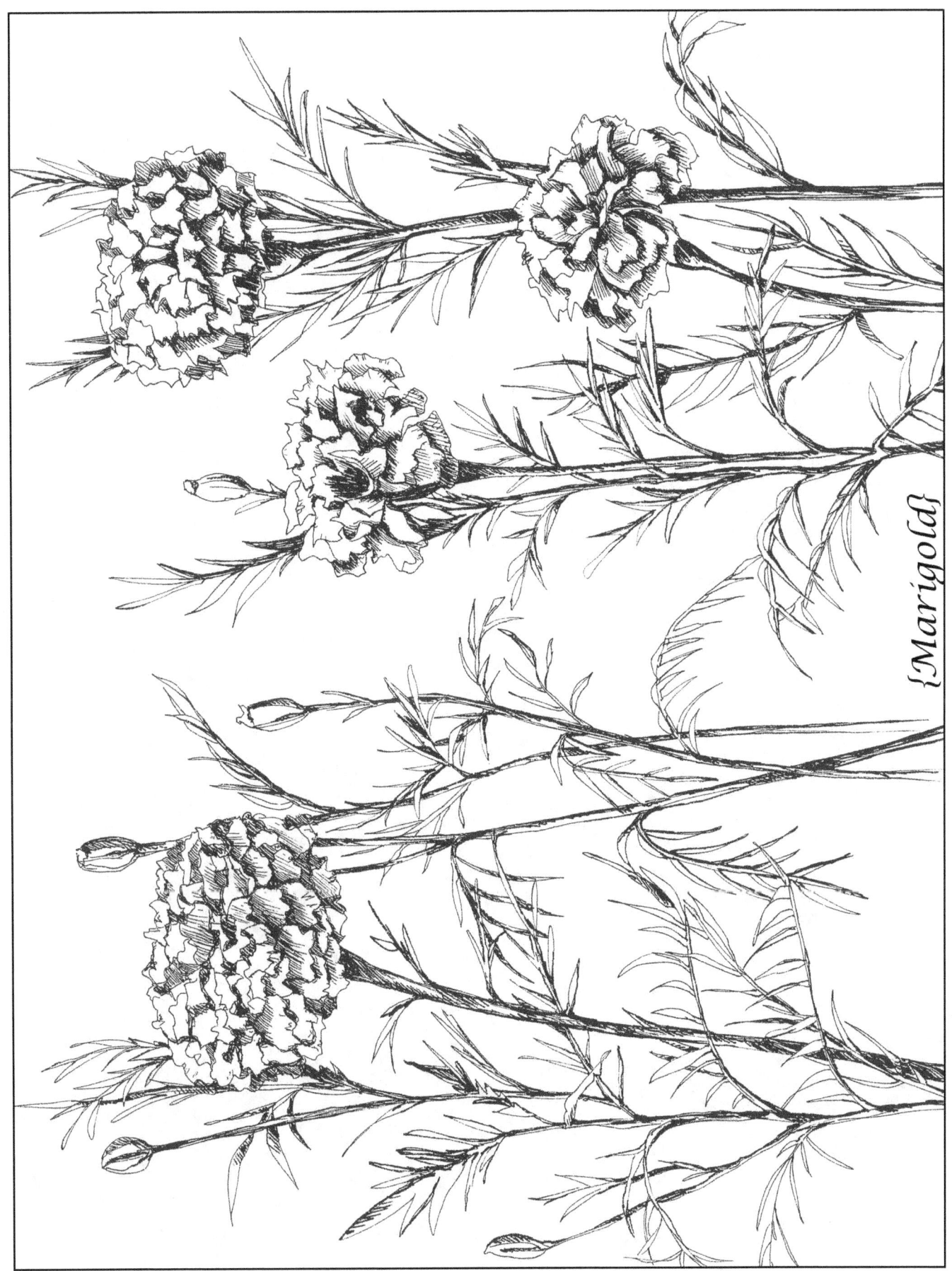

{Marigold}

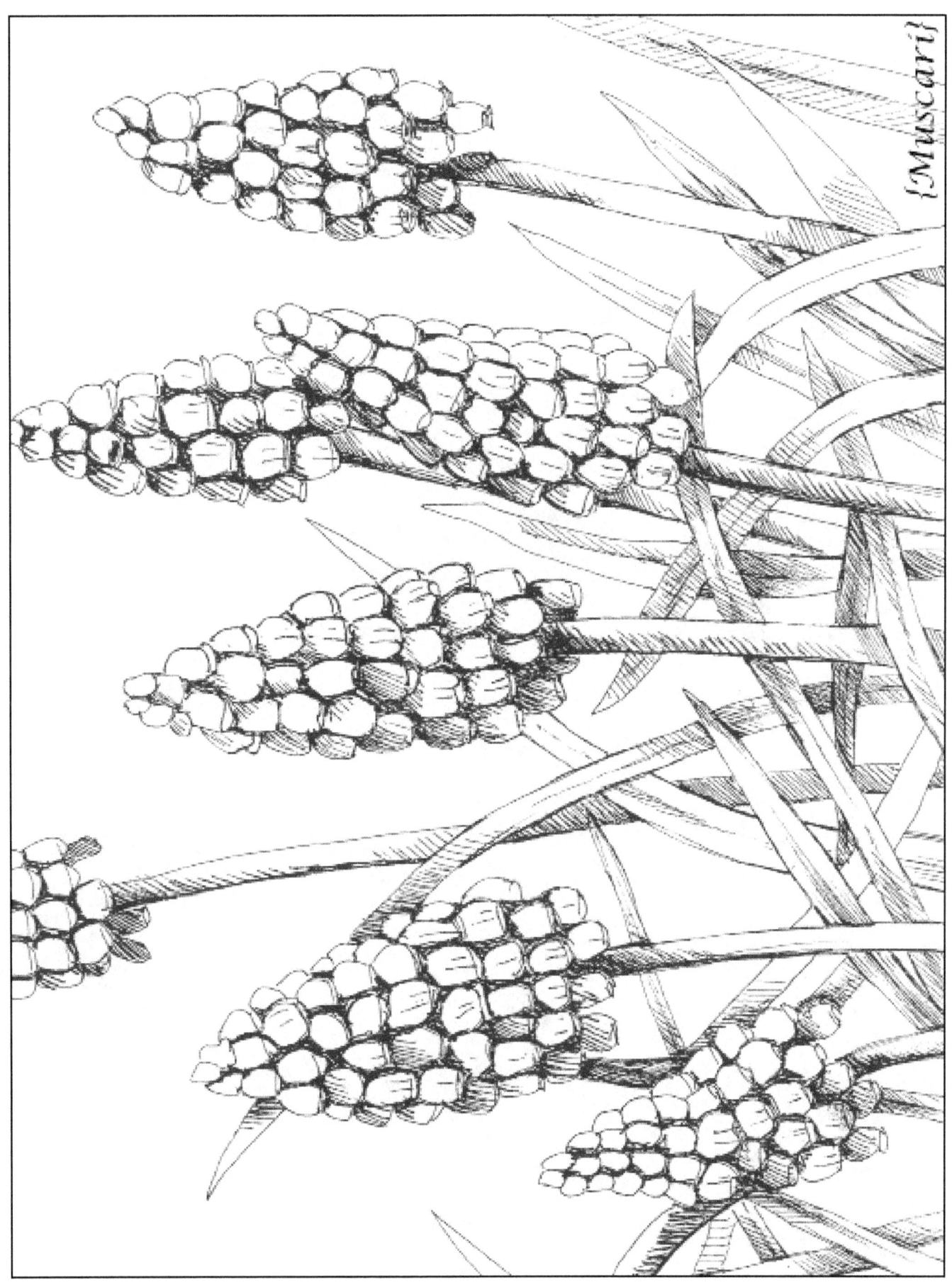

{Muscari}

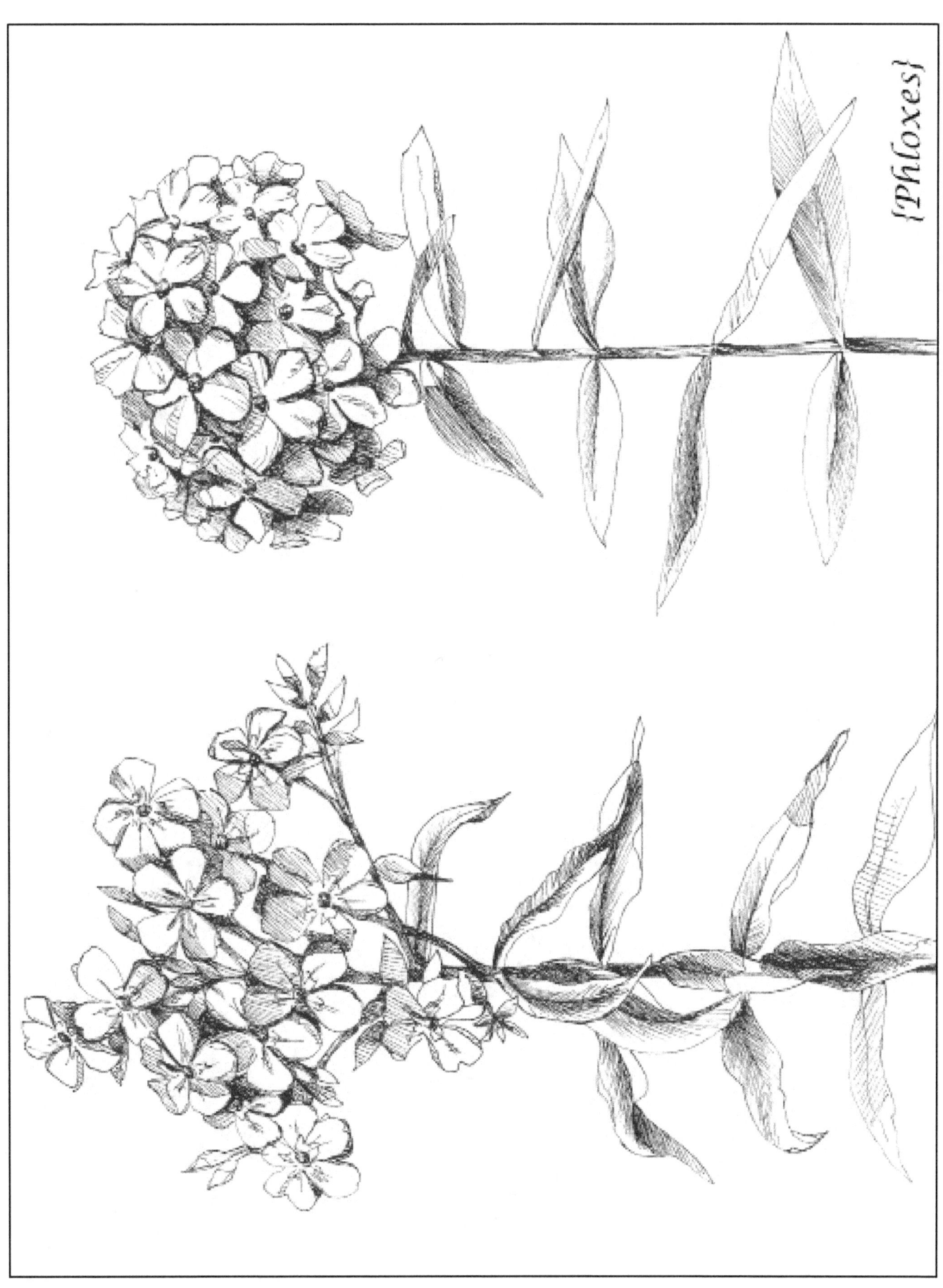

{Phloxes}

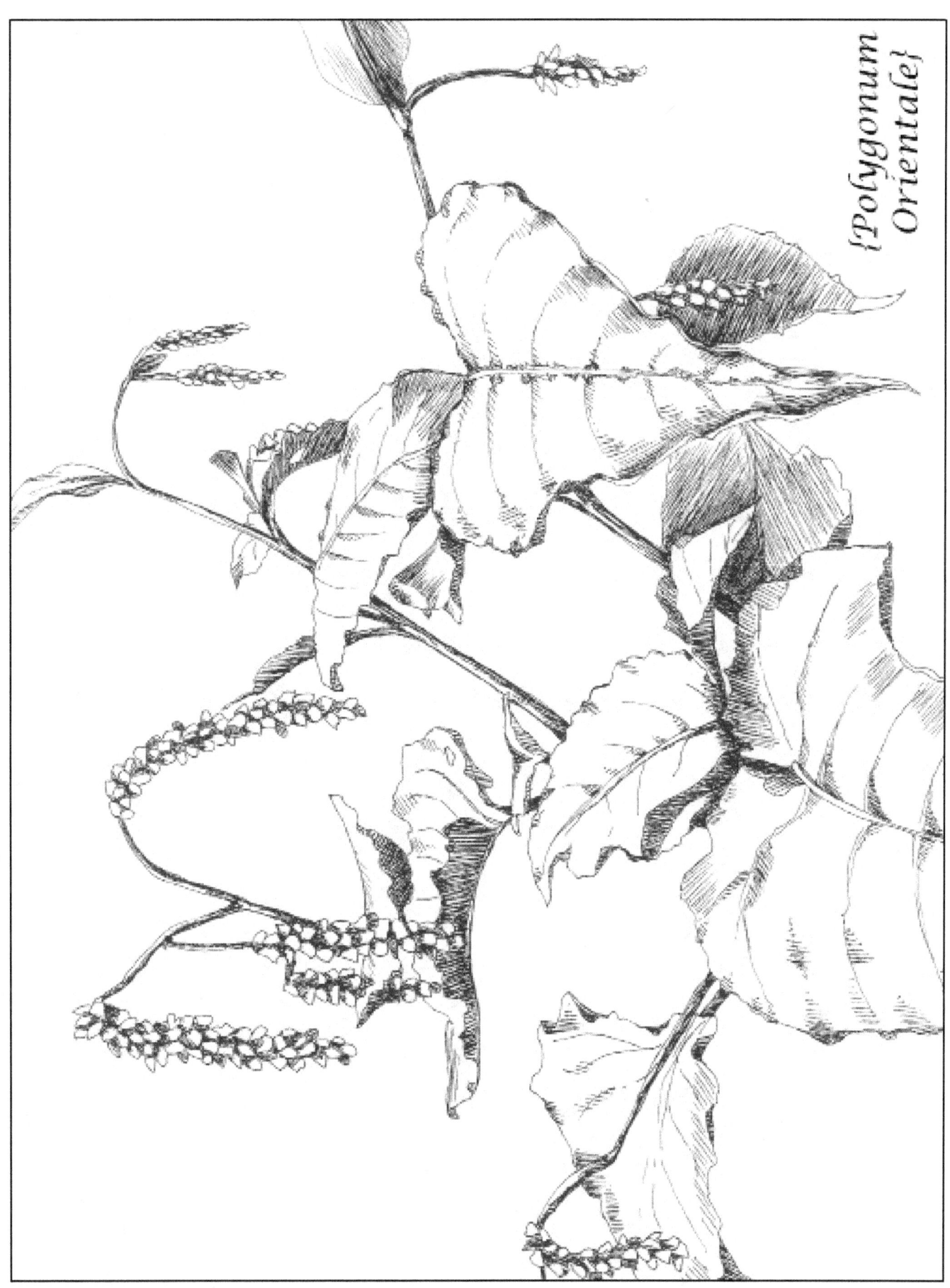

{Polygonum Orientale}

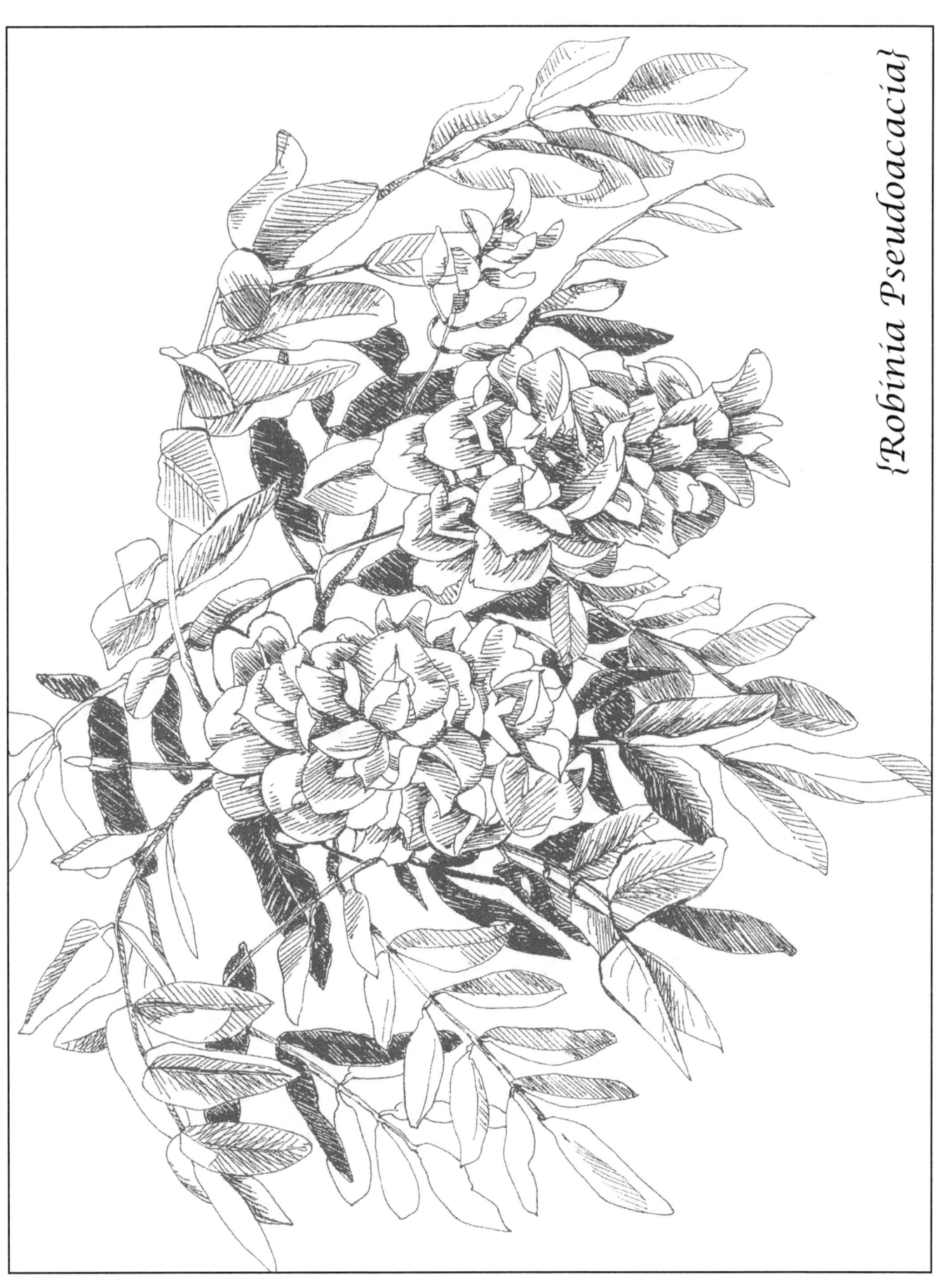

{Robinia Pseudoacacia}

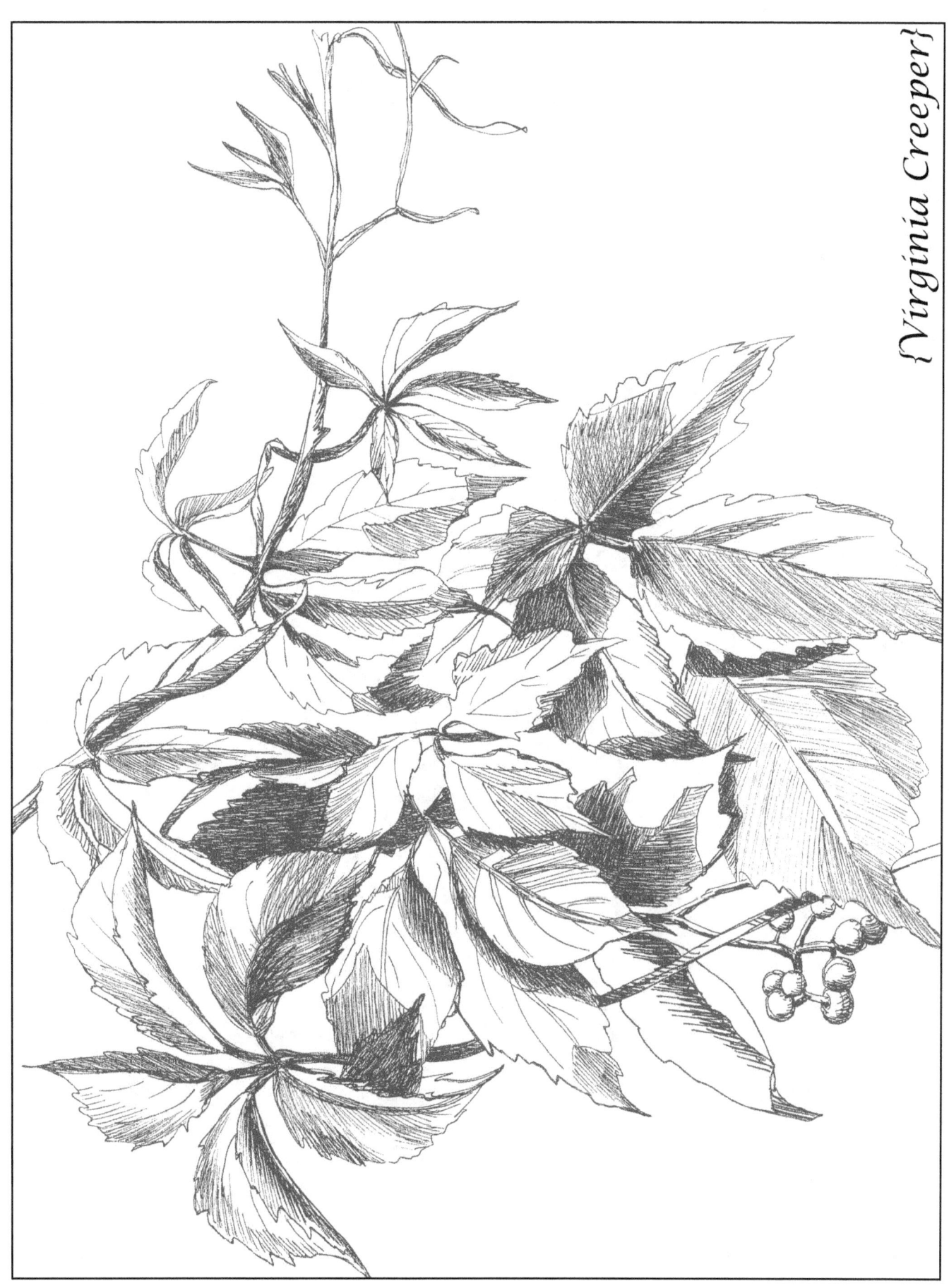

{Virginia Creeper}

MAKE AN ARTIST HAPPY TODAY

So, here is the end of the Flowers Coloring Book For Adults. Thank you for buying my book.

If you found the coloring book fun and helpful, I'd be grateful if you took a few minutes to write a review on Amazon.
When you post a review, it makes a huge difference to help new colorists find my coloring books.
Your review would make my day!

Thank you,
Viktoriya

MY FREE GIFT FOR YOU

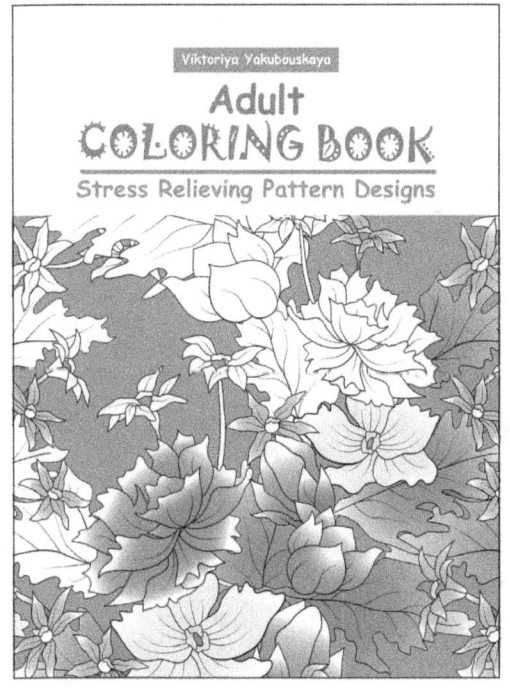

Get a PDF coloring book to help you relax and have fun with your creative hobby for FREE:

Adult Coloring Book: Stress Relieving Pattern Designs

Join my email list and get this e-book. The coloring can be downloaded as a file your computer or added to any device. You will also receive my e-newsletter with news, special offers, freebies occasionally.

Download this coloring for free today at:
http://bit.ly/my-books-list

Check out my other coloring books - https://amazon.com/author/viktoriya-ya

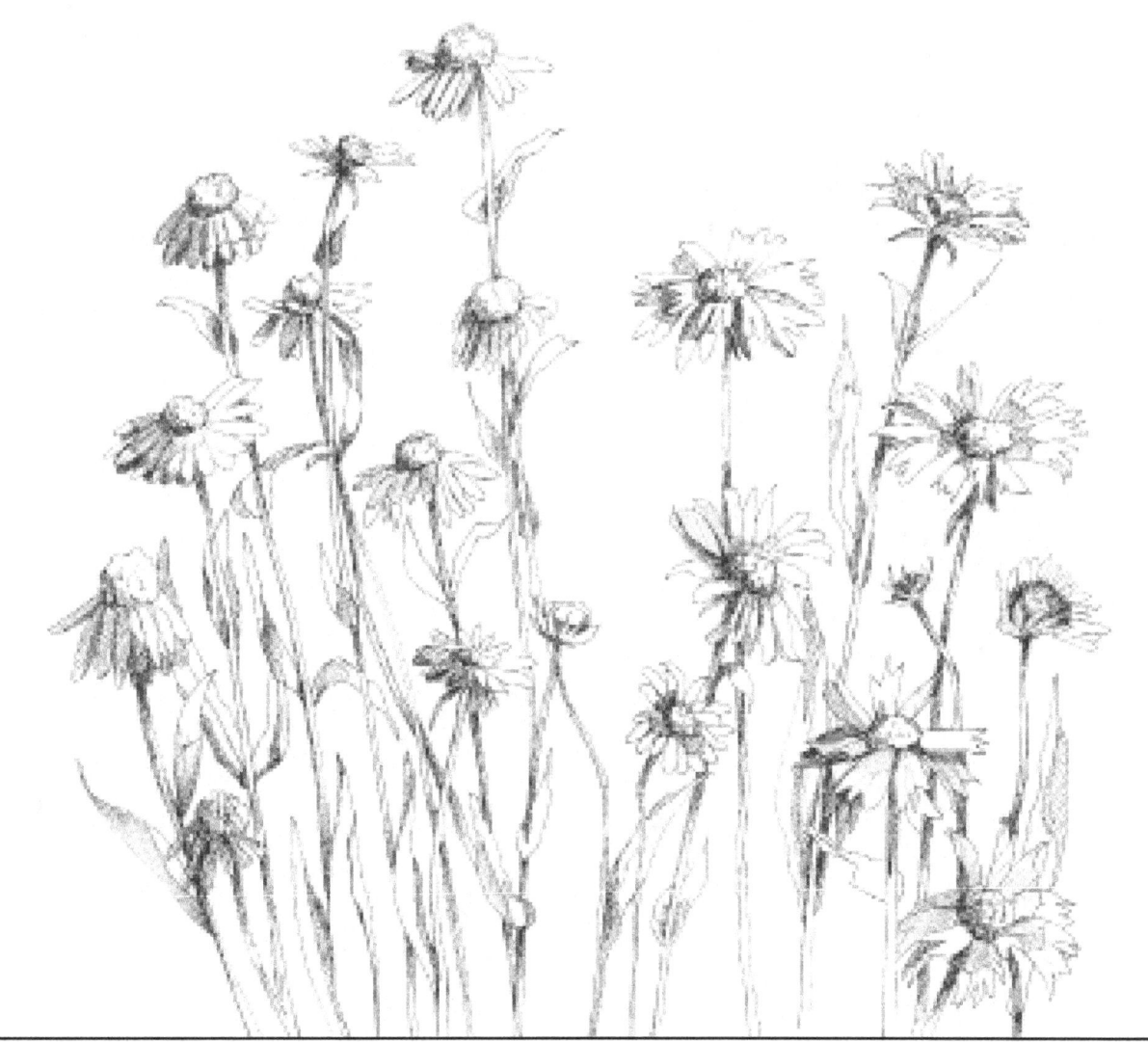

www.ingramcontent.com/pod-product-compliance
Lightning Source LLC
Chambersburg PA
CBHW081524220526
45467CB00010B/3032

* 9 7 8 1 7 1 1 2 3 0 5 3 5 *